ALWAYS
TRUE

God's Promises When Life Is Hard

JAMES
MACDONALD

LifeWay Press®
Nashville, Tennessee

Published by LifeWay Press®
© 2011 James MacDonald

No part of this book may be reproduced or transmitted in any form or by any means, electronic or mechanical, including photocopying and recording or by any information storage or retrieval system, except as may be expressly permitted in writing by the publisher. Requests for permission should be addressed in writing to LifeWay Press®; One LifeWay Plaza; Nashville, TN; 37234-0175.

ISBN 978-1-4158-6989-5
Item 005371573

Dewey decimal classification: 231.7
Subject headings: GOD—PROMISES \ CHRISTIAN LIFE

Unless otherwise stated, all Scripture quotations are taken from The Holy Bible, English Standard Version, copyright © 2000, 2001 by Crossway Bibles, a division of Good News Publishers. Scripture quotations marked NKJV are taken from the New King James Version. Copyright © 1979, 1980, 1982, Thomas Nelson Inc., Publishers. Scripture quotations marked NASB are taken from the New American Standard Bible®, Copyright © 1960, 1962, 1963, 1971, 1972, 1973, 1974, 1977, 1995 by the Lockman Foundation. Used by permission. *(www.lockman.org)* Scripture quotations marked NIV are taken from the Holy Bible, New International Version. copyright © 1973, 1978, 1984 by International Bible Society.

To order additional copies of this resource, write to LifeWay Church Resources Customer Service; One LifeWay Plaza; Nashville, TN 37234-0113; fax (615) 251-5933; phone toll free (800) 458-2772; e-mail *orderentry@lifeway.com;* order online at *www.lifeway.com;* or visit a LifeWay Christian Store.

Printed in the United States of America

Leadership and Adult Publishing
LifeWay Church Resources
One Life Way Plaza
Nashville, TN 37234-0175

Fruit of the Spirit
Beth Moore

CONTENTS

THE AUTHOR

 James MacDonald is the founding and senior pastor of Harvest Bible Chapel in the northwestern suburbs of Chicago, Illinois. Harvest Bible Chapel is a church based on prayer, boldness in evangelism, Spirit-filled worship, and the unapologetic proclamation of God's Word. In its first two decades Harvest has grown to more than 12,000 members. Additionally, it has sent out more than 1,000 leaders to launch 15 new churches with more than 8,000 in attendance.

James's teaching can be heard on the daily, 30-minute radio program *Walk in the Word*, which airs across North America. The mission of *Walk in the Word* is to ignite passion in God's people through the proclamation of biblical truth.

Born in London, Ontario, Canada, James received his master's degree from Trinity Evangelical Divinity School in Deerfield, Illinois, and his doctorate from Phoenix Seminary. He and his wife, Kathy, have three adult children and reside in Chicago.

For more information about James and these ministries, visit *www.harvestbible.org* or *www.walkintheword.com*.

Other Books by James MacDonald

Always True: God's Five Promises for When Life Is Hard (Moody Publishers, 2011)
Ancient Wisdom (B&H Publishing Group, 2006)
Downpour: He Will Come to Us like the Rain small-group study (LifeWay Press, 2006)
Downpour: He Will Come to Us like the Rain (B&H Publishing Group, 2006)
God Wrote a Book (Crossway Books, 2002)
Gripped by the Greatness of God small-group study (LifeWay Press, 2005)
Gripped by the Greatness of God (Moody Publishers, 2005)
I Really Want to Change . . . So, Help Me God (Moody Publishers, 2000)
Lord, Change My Attitude small-group study (LifeWay Press, 2008)
Lord, Change My Attitude . . . Before It's Too Late (Moody Publishers, 2001)
Seven Words to Change Your Family (Moody Publishers, 2001)
When Life Is Hard small-group study (LifeWay Press, 2010)
When Life Is Hard (Moody Publishers, 2010)

Visit *www.lifeway.com/jamesmacdonald* for information about James MacDonald resources published by LifeWay.

INTRODUCTION

Always True comes to you life-tested. In the weeks to come, we are going to look at five special and powerful promises of God that have stood the judgment of history. The people who first received these promises and countless others who have followed in their steps could testify, "God has kept His Word. These promises proved true in our lives, and they will always be true." This study will give you an opportunity to personally test God's promises by applying them to the problems and trials you are experiencing in your life.

Here are the promises we will study.

1. I will not fear; God is always with me.
2. I will not doubt; God is always in control.
3. I will not despair; God is always good.
4. I will not falter; God is always watching.
5. I will not fail; God is always victorious.

In the first week of our study we will look at God as the great Promise Keeper. Because He is trustworthy, we can trust His promises. Then in weeks 2–6 we will look at the five promises to learn how they will change our perspective on our life circumstances.

The apostle Peter wrote that God has "granted to us his precious and very great promises, so that through them you may become partakers of the divine nature, having escaped from the corruption that is in the world because of sinful desire" (2 Pet. 1:4). If we take God's promises to heart, we will find them to be our greatest resources for fighting the battles of this life and for embracing a walk of ever-growing faith. When God's promises prove to be effective and true, they become precious to us.

No matter what you are going through, your situation would look very different in the light of God's promises. Get to know the great promises in God's Word. When life is hard, you can count on them to be always true.

How to Get the Most from This Study

1. **Attend each group experience.**
   - Watch the DVD teaching.
   - Participate in the group discussion.
2. **Complete the daily assignments in this workbook.**
   - Read the material.
   - Complete the learning activities.
   - Memorize each week's memory verse. Scripture-memory cards are provided at the back.
   - Watch for God to fulfill His promises in your life.

THE THEOLOGY OF PROMISE

God's Promises

I will not fear; God is always with me.

I will not doubt; God is always in control.

I will not despair; God is always good.

I will not falter; God is always watching.

I will not fail; God is always victorious.

This Week's Memory Verses

"His divine power has granted to us all things that pertain to life and godliness, through the knowledge of him who called us to his own glory and excellence, by which he has granted to us his precious and very great promises, so that through them you may become partakers of the divine nature, having escaped from the corruption that is in the world because of sinful desire."

2 Peter 1:3-4

It's All About God

Niagara Falls is the honeymoon capital of the world. Each year thousands of newlyweds visit this breathtaking site to celebrate their marriages. One of the most magnificent sites, Horseshoe Falls, is 2,600 feet around the rim and 167 feet high. More than six hundred thousand gallons of water flow over the falls every second.

God has said in His Word,

> "Deep calls to deep
> at the roar of your waterfalls;
> all your breakers and your waves
> have gone over me." *Psalm 42:7*

Scripture frequently paints vivid pictures like this to proclaim God's creative power. God literally spoke the universe into existence. We're about to study five of God's very great promises, so it's appropriate that we begin with a reminder of His creative majesty. If God has the power to speak and form the universe, He has the power to keep all of the promises He has made to us in His Word.

In this first week we will focus on the theology of God's promises. *Theology* means *words about God* or *God words,* so *theology of promise* means we will examine God's words about His promises. This means we will learn not only what God says about His promises but also what God's promises tell us about Him. If we want to understand the theology of promise, we have to start with God.

Think of God's promises as an all-access backstage pass to Scripture's greatest treasures, giving you a behind-the-curtain view of God's plans for the Christian walk. They will be your light when the way is darkest. They will produce hope, strength, and confidence to lift your heavy burdens. When nothing else makes sense, these promises will literally hold you up and carry you forward to better days that are coming. I am assured of this because the promises come from God Himself. That's why our first week of study will focus on the character of the God who stands behind the promises. A guarantee doesn't mean much unless the party issuing the guarantee has the resources to deliver what was promised. Believe me: God can deliver. He is reliable. He is eternal. He is faithful. Therefore, His promises are always true.

GROUP EXPERIENCE

On the Same Page

If you are meeting as a group for the first time, introduce one another. Share your responses to the following.

- Identify groups, organizations, and institutions that are known for not being trustworthy.
- List promotional messages you see or hear that instantly cause you to think, *That can't be true.*
- Share examples of broken promises in today's culture that you have observed or experienced.

Preparation

1. When you heard this study would examine God's promises, what was the first thought that went through your mind?

2. What promises of God already hold special meaning for you?

3. Together read aloud this week's memory verses on page 6.

DVD Session 1 Viewer Guide

God is by nature a _____.

Promise: an assurance God gives His people so that they can _____ by _____ while they wait for Him to _____

God's promises are _____ (see 2 Pet. 1:3-4).

1. God's promises come from a great _____.
2. God's promises cover the great _____.
3. God's promises bring us great _____.
4. God's promises lead to a great _____.

God's promises are _____ great (see 2 Pet. 1:3-4).

1. Greater than _____ _____
2. Greater than white-knuckled _____
3. Greater than _____ in self-pity

God's promises are exceedingly great and _____ (see 2 Pet. 1:3-4).

Precious things take:
1. _____
2. _____

Two kinds of promises in the Bible:

1. A _____ covenant
2. An _____ covenant
Covenant: a sworn _____ between two parties

God is a _____.

God _____ His promises.

God wants us to _____ His promises.

Don't act _____ and expect God to _____ you out.
Don't act _____ and provoke God to _____ you.

God's promises are activated by _____.

The promise is never real to you until:
1. You _____ it.
2. You _____ it.
3. You _____ it.

God's promises are experienced in _____ _____.

Responding to the DVD Teaching

1. In what ways would you say God is precious to you today?

2. Look at the definition of *promise* in your viewer guide (p. 8).
How would you express that definition in your own words?

3. What examples can you think of in your own experiences of the
"Today I believe; tomorrow I receive" principle?

Read week 2 and complete the activities before the next group experience. Read and recite this week's memory verses, 2 Peter 1:3-4, at least once each day this week.

This video session is available for download at *www.lifeway.com/alwaystrue.*

GOD MAKES PROMISES

Today's Scripture Focus

"He has granted to us his precious and very great promises, so that through them you may become partakers of the divine nature, having escaped from the corruption that is in the world because of sinful desire."
2 Peter 1:4

I remember with stark vividness some incredibly dark days. With trembling hands and a desperate heart, I began to search the Scriptures, knowing I could grope my way to the light if I could just find some promises to hold on to. God's Word is like a mountain of gold, and when we dig in the mountain, we continually discover His promises shining like diamonds.

Read the following examples of promises God has made to us in His Word. Check any that speak to needs in your life at this time.

"Be strong and courageous. Do not fear or be in dread of them,
for it is the Lord your God who goes with you.
He will not leave you or forsake you." *Deuteronomy 31:6*

"They who wait for the Lord shall renew their strength;
they shall mount up with wings like eagles;
they shall run and not be weary;
they shall walk and not faint." *Isaiah 40:31*

"I know the plans I have for you, declares the Lord, plans for welfare
and not for evil, to give you a future and a hope." *Jeremiah 29:11*

"If you ask me anything in my name, I will do it." *John 14:14*

"Peace I leave with you; my peace I give to you.
Not as the world gives do I give to you. Let not your hearts
be troubled, neither let them be afraid." *John 14:27*

"My God will supply every need of yours according
to his riches in glory in Christ Jesus." *Philippians 4:19*

God's Word is like a mountain of gold, and when we dig in the mountain, we continually discover His promises shining like diamonds.

"For those who love God all things work together for good,
for those who are called according to his purpose." *Romans 8:28*

"If we confess our sins, he is faithful and just to forgive our sins
and to cleanse us from all unrighteousness." *1 John 1:9*

God Is a Promiser

The Bible reveals a God who makes promises. He is a promiser by nature. A general definition of *promise* is *a declaration of what someone will do.* A promise from God is an assurance He gives His people that enables them to walk by faith while they wait for Him to work. With a promise God first gives us a picture of what will come about. Then He gives us the real thing. He tells us what He is going to do, and then He does what He said He would do. In the meantime our job is to walk by faith in what God has promised to do. Today we believe; tomorrow we receive. When God promises something, you can believe and act on it.

The very idea that God commits Himself to do anything is incredible. He doesn't have to bind Himself to us in any way. He is God—completely above and beyond us. Yet He promises to do certain things for us. And He has recorded those promises in His Word to give us hope no matter what trials and hardships we are going through. Even when it's hard to trust God during these times, His promises remain the same. Nothing can change God's stated intent. He has not left us wondering what is going to happen, uncertain about the future, or overcome by fear. He has given us promises as assurances of the outcomes of those dark and difficult times when life is hard.

Check the statement that most closely describes the way you relate to God's promises.

☐ God's promises are hopeful ideas that make me feel good.
☐ God's promises are for others, not for me.
☐ God's promises are central to the way I live my life.
☐ God's promises are something I rarely think about.

Are you accustomed to looking at God's promises as an assurance—a sure thing? How does this perspective affect your confidence in God's Word?

How do you think God's promises help believers walk by faith?

Today we believe; tomorrow we receive.

Every moment of the Christian journey is a walk of faith. When you walk by faith, you believe there will be a day when God will fulfill His Word. All that stands between you and what He has promised is time. His promises give us something to hang on to during the long wait. The hardest part of hanging on is the gap between believing His promise and receiving the fulfillment of that promise. The Christian life would be easy if the time were short between our appeal to God's promises and our receiving what He promised. But life isn't like that. We have to wait without knowing the outcome or how long the wait will be.

What trials or difficulties are you waiting through now? How are they affecting your faith in God?

What role are God's promises playing during your wait?

The wait is where God's promises come in. We must review His promises all the time. We must remind ourselves that our faith is in God and not in what He does for us. He knows what He has promised. He can't lie, and He can't forget. He will deliver on time all the time. His promises allow us to hang on to His Word. While we wait, we learn to trust God, and He builds our faith.

God's promises allow us to hang on to His Word.

In general, we can classify God's promises in Scripture as foundational or functional. Foundational promises apply to God's plans for history and all humankind. Functional promises, on the other hand, are those we can apply to our personal lives and our walk with Christ.

Read the following verses and indicate whether they represent foundational or functional promises.

Genesis 3:15	☐ Foundational	☐ Functional
Genesis 9:11	☐ Foundational	☐ Functional
Genesis 12:2-3	☐ Foundational	☐ Functional
John 3:16	☐ Foundational	☐ Functional
Philippians 4:19	☐ Foundational	☐ Functional
James 1:12	☐ Foundational	☐ Functional

Precious and Great Promises

Today's Scripture focus, 2 Peter 1:4, says God "has granted to us his precious and very great promises, so that through them you may become partakers of the divine nature, having escaped from the corruption that is in the world because of sinful desire."

What two adjectives did Peter use to describe God's promises?

What is the goal of God's promises in a believer's life?

God's promises are great. God's promises are great because they come from a great God. Jeremiah 32:27 quotes God as saying, "I am the LORD, the God of all flesh. Is anything too hard for me?" Sometimes we look at our need or our overwhelming circumstance and feel defeated. However, our promise-keeping God says, "Nothing is too hard for Me." Holding on to God's promises is the next best thing to holding on to God.

God's promises are great because they address the great issues—life, sin, death, good, evil, fear, despair, hope, purpose. You can search the Bible for answers to the biggest issues you will ever face.

God's promises are greater than anything else available to us. They are greater than human wisdom. Proverbs 18:2 says,

> "A fool takes no pleasure in understanding,
> but only in expressing his opinion."

When it comes down to it, human wisdom is just a matter of our own opinions. But God has spoken, and He has made promises to those who choose to love and trust Him. We need to get on board with what He has promised in His Word.

God's promises are greater than white-knuckled obedience. Have you ever been hit with a problem so big that all you can think to do is hang on? *I'm going to get through this. If I can just hang on, this is going to work itself out.* Rather than endure our trials like an endless marathon, we can rely on God's promises to give us peace and confidence during the wait.

God's promises are greater than wallowing in self-pity. Some people get hit with a wave of difficulty that is followed by a tsunami of self-pity. That's an

> **Holding on to God's promises is the next best thing to holding on to God.**

understandable initial reaction, but after that we need to rise to the surface, take hold of the promises of God, and ride those waves to shore.

God's promises are precious. *Precious* is not a kindergarten word. When you're young, you don't know what is valuable. But the older you get, the more you realize that precious takes time.

> **Read the following verses and write the things or people Peter described as precious.**
>
> 1 Peter 1:7:
>
> 1 Peter 1:19:
>
> 1 Peter 2:4:
>
> 1 Peter 2:6:

Peter used the word *precious* to describe what is most valuable in the kingdom of God. As we believe and act on God's great and precious promises, He leads us out of sin to become "partakers of the divine nature" (2 Pet. 1:4), the righteous character of Christ.

Owning God's Promises

Beginning in week 2, we will study five major promises God has made.

1. I will not fear; God is always with me.
2. I will not doubt; God is always in control.
3. I will not despair; God is always good.
4. I will not falter; God is always watching.
5. I will not fail; God is always victorious.

> **Underline the promise above that you find most reassuring at this time in your life.**

These five promises all require responses from us. We have to be willing to let them work in our lives. This is why we must set aside our expectations of instant gratification when it comes to God's promises. We actively trust a promise and then wait for God to follow through on that promise. Today we believe; tomorrow (or at some point in the future) we receive. God determines the timing of His promises; we don't.

God determines the timing of His promises; we don't.

I wish I could tell you God's promises always work out perfectly in our lifetimes, but that isn't always the case. God's promises are not just for this life. You must factor eternity into the equation. Heaven will bring the whole story together.

David made a powerful statement of faith in Psalm 27:13 (NKJV):

> "I would have lost heart, unless I had believed
> That I would see the goodness of the LORD
> In the land of the living."

Some promises are for heaven, beyond this life. We may want to see them now; only then are we going to see them. But notice that David didn't hang his hopes on a particular promise and hold God to a narrow expectation: "Unless You do this specific thing for me, God, I won't keep trusting You." He opened his eyes wide to let God show him His goodness "in the land of the living."

Hebrews 6:11-12 tells us we must persevere in light of God's promises: "We desire each one of you to show the same earnestness to have the full assurance of hope until the end, so that you may not be sluggish, but imitators of those who through faith and patience inherit the promises." God doesn't want one person to quit. He puts promises in our hands so that we can grow in our faith, demonstrating the authenticity of a life lived in Christ.

God puts promises in our hands so that we can grow in our faith.

What hardships and trials are you struggling with?

Would observers be able to say you are striving with earnestness and with the full assurance of hope? ☐ Yes ☐ No

Pray and ask God to use this study to increase your faith as you learn to trust His promises.

Begin memorizing this week's memory verses, 2 Peter 1:3-4. Scripture-memory cards are provided at the back of your workbook.

GOD KEEPS HIS PROMISES

Today's Scripture Focus

"We desire each one of you to show the same earnestness to have the full assurance of hope until the end, so that you may not be sluggish, but imitators of those who through faith and patience inherit the promises. For when God made a promise to Abraham, since he had no one greater by whom to swear, he swore by himself, saying, 'Surely I will bless you and multiply you.' And thus Abraham, having patiently waited, obtained the promise. For people swear by something greater than themselves, and in all their disputes an oath is final for confirmation. So when God desired to show more convincingly to the heirs of the promise the unchangeable character of his purpose, he guaranteed it with an oath, so that by two unchangeable things, in which it is impossible for God to lie, we who have fled for refuge might have strong encouragement to hold fast to the hope set before us."

Hebrews 6:11-18

Today's Scripture focus gives us not only a central promise of Scripture but also insight into the character of the One behind the promise—God Himself. If we are continually moving toward a clearer understanding of God as He has revealed Himself in Scripture, we can experience the assurance His promises were designed to bring about in our lives. The solid foundation on which the Christian life rests is the conviction that God will keep His promises. In our walk with Christ, we need to keep going—keep loving, serving, obeying—until we get what God promised. We don't have all He promised yet. In fact, we don't have even the smallest fraction of it. There is so much yet to come. We have to press on and wait in faith, and someday He will fulfill all He said He would do.

> **The solid foundation on which the Christian life rests is the conviction that God will keep His promises.**

The Ultimate Promise Keeper

You and I may have the most noble of intentions, but our best promise means "I want to; I intend to; I'll try my best." Only time will tell whether we keep our promise. It's not like that with God. When God promises, He's not saying, "I'll try." He means "I can, and I will!" Who else can say that? A well-intentioned home buyer takes out a loan but may not make good on it. The bank tries to insure the loan, but as our nation learned during the first decade of the 21st century, even large financial institutions can't always come through on what they commit to do.

Identify a time when you were not able to keep a promise you made to someone or someone failed to keep a promise to you.

We can't allow our disappointments with the uncertainties of living in a fallen world to destroy the assurance we have in God.

What caused the failure to follow through?

We can't allow our disappointments with the uncertainties of living in a fallen world to destroy the assurance we have in God. When all around us people are breaking their word, we can hold on to the truth that God keeps His promises!

Read the following pairs of verses. Record the way God's promise in the first verse(s) of the pair was fulfilled in the second verse(s) of the pair.

Scriptures	Fulfillment
Genesis 12:1-3; Joshua 21:43	
2 Samuel 6:12-13; Luke 2:11	
Jeremiah 29:10; Ezra 1:1-4	
Acts 1:8; 2:1-4	

Inheriting the Promises

In the Old Testament many promises God made to people were known as covenants. A covenant is a formal promise. The Bible contains two kinds of covenant promises.

1. A conditional covenant includes our part and God's part. We do our part; then God does His. The Mosaic covenant given in Exodus 19–24, including the Ten Commandments, is an example of a conditional promise. In short, God said, "If you obey Me, you will be blessed. If you disobey, you will be judged."

2. An unconditional covenant involves only God. He carries the weight of both parties. God says, "I'm going to make this promise based on My character alone. You don't have to do anything." We don't have to meet any conditions to realize this promise.

Read Genesis 12:1-3 and underline God's promises to Abraham.

"The LORD said to Abram, 'Go from your country and your kindred and your father's house to the land that I will show you. And I will make of you a great nation, and I will bless you and make your name great,

so that you will be a blessing. I will bless those who bless you,
and him who dishonors you I will curse, and in you
all the families of the earth shall be blessed.' "

Which type of covenant was this? ☐ **Conditional** ☐ **Unconditional**

The covenant between God and Abraham was an unconditional covenant. God chose a people for Himself while only the future father of the nation was there to witness God's promise.

A covenant is a serious commitment. The word *covenant* actually means *to make a cut.* In the Old Testament the two parties involved in the covenant had a ceremony. They took a sacrificial animal, killed it, and cut it in half lengthwise. Then they separated the animal on the ground, stood between the two halves, shook hands, and swore that whatever they had committed to do would be done, sealing the deal. When God made an unconditional covenant with Abraham, He went through the whole ceremony by Himself. He put Abraham to sleep and stood alone between the pieces of the sacrificial animal, signifying that He would fulfill this commitment no matter what Abraham did (see Gen. 15:1-21).

In our Scripture focus today the writer of Hebrews used the covenant with Abraham as an example of God's faithfulness that we can depend on. Abraham hung on to God's promise, patiently walking by faith, and saw God working out His word through his son Isaac and his place in the promised land. "Abraham, having patiently waited, obtained the promise" (Heb. 6:15).

Hebrews 6:17-18 says God guaranteed His promise to Abraham with an oath tied to "two unchangeable things":

1. His character—who God is
2. His Word—what God says

Because of the unchangeable nature of God's character and His Word, God's promise to Abraham could not change.

Because of the unchangeable nature of God's character and His Word, God's promise to Abraham could not change. The same is true of His promises to us—all of the promises in His Word. In our human nature it's hard for us even to imagine unchangeable. We've never experienced anything so secure and solid. Jesus told us, "Heaven and earth will pass away, but my words will not pass away" (Matt. 24:35). No one but God can make a claim like that—and keep it! These are unchangeable words from an unchangeable God: "Jesus Christ is the same yesterday and today and forever" (Heb. 13:8).

How do these unchangeable things give you confidence in God's promises?

God's unchanging character:

God's unchanging Word:

Check the areas of life in which you are patiently waiting to see God work out His promises.

☐ Personal spiritual life   ☐ Ministry
☐ Marriage   ☐ Church
☐ Family life   ☐ Trial or hardship
☐ Vocation
☐ Other:

Describe the way you are exercising faith in at least one of these areas as you wait for God to keep His promises.

In giving us His promises, God wants us to show "the same earnestness to have the full assurance of hope until the end, so that you may not be sluggish, but imitators of those who through faith and patience inherit the promises" (Heb. 6:11-12). Like Abraham, Isaac, Jacob, and Joseph, we can look with faith to the time God's promises come true.

> **We can look with faith to the time God's promises come true.**

God is not only able but also willing to keep His promises to us. Read Romans 8:32 and underline what God desires to give us.

"He who did not spare his own Son but gave him up for us all,
how will he not also with him graciously give us all things?"

Identify a specific issue or problem in your life for which you need a promise.

Ask God to show you a Scripture promise that speaks to this issue. Write it here.

Claim this verse as God's promise to you. Ask God to give you faith in His character and His Word as you wait for Him to keep His promise.

Work on your memory verses for this week, 2 Peter 1:3-4.

GOD WANTS US TO TEST HIS PROMISES

Today's Scripture Focus

"Your promise is well tried,
and your servant loves it." *Psalm 119:140*

"Not one word of all the good promises that the LORD had made
to the house of Israel had failed; all came to pass." *Joshua 21:45*

"Blessed be the LORD who has given rest to his people Israel, according
to all that he promised. Not one word has failed of all his good
promise, which he spoke by Moses his servant." *1 Kings 8:56*

If you are a regular radio listener, you are used to those occasional interruptions that say, "The following is a test of the emergency broadcast system. ... This is only a test." You may have lived your entire life without ever hearing that announcement changed to "This is the emergency broadcast system. This is not a test; it is a real emergency!" Although we may not appreciate having our favorite song or program interrupted, we recognize the value of testing a system that was designed to alert us in case of an emergency.

God's promises are designed to be tested.

Our Scripture focus for today reminds us that God's promises are designed to be tested. They are tried commitments, meaning that when they were needed, they proved dependable. The background of the word *try*, when used in this sense, includes a technical term from forging that described the process of testing a metal for purity and strength. This is the beautiful meaning of the word *tried* in a comforting verse like Job 23:10:

"He knows the way that I take;
when he has tried me, I shall come out as gold."

We don't have to come up with artificial breaks in our programming to test God's promises. Life will present us with plenty of real-life moments when we can observe ways God lives up to His Word. If we are watching, we will be able to say with the psalmist,

> "Your promise is well tried,
> and your servant loves it." *Psalm 119:140*

When we make promises, we often include some unspoken small print that is filled with *if* clauses: *I will do this if the creek doesn't rise, if I feel like it, if it doesn't interfere with other plans, if I don't get a better offer, if there aren't unexpected complications.* That's one way we are different from God. He already knows there will be real difficulties, but He makes His promises anyway. He doesn't make promises you won't need. He expects you to be at a crossroads where you have to lean on Him; where you must rest on His promises; and where you are ready to claim them, hold them, and treasure them in your heart. God flat-out wants you to test His promises.

God doesn't make promises you won't need.

Identify one of God's promises you have tried in your life. How would you describe the outcome of that test?

Every person who knows and loves the Lord will experience circumstances in which they have no option but to put God's promises to the test. There's simply nowhere else to turn. Every other prop is going to be removed until we can go forward only on our confidence in God's promises. Every time we test those promises, God will prove Himself true.

Tried Promises

The biblical account of Israel's journey to the promised land contains multiple examples of God's faithfulness to His promises. After the miraculous delivery from Egypt and the 40-year training tour through the wilderness, the people had finally entered the land. Moses had passed off the scene, and his replacement, Joshua, reminded the people of the many promises that had proved true along the way: "Not one word of all the good promises that the LORD had made to the house of Israel had failed; all came to pass" (Josh. 21:45). Realizing there was still a lot of work to do to possess the land, Joshua understood that when he was gone from the scene, the diligence of the people might flag. He wanted to remind them that God had been faithful to His promises and assured them they could go forward confident of His continued faithfulness. He issued this challenge: "If it is evil in your eyes to serve the LORD, choose this day whom you will serve, whether the gods your fathers served in the region beyond the River, or the gods of the Amorites in whose land you dwell. But as for me and my house, we will serve the LORD" (Josh. 24:15).

Many years later Solomon, a son of David, had inherited and consolidated the kingdom of Israel in the largest and most settled form it would ever achieve. The hard-fought victories of David had left Solomon with a kingdom of peace. As Solomon dedicated the great temple in Jerusalem, he proclaimed God's fulfillment of all of His promises: "Blessed be the LORD who has given rest to his people Israel, according to all that he promised. Not one word has failed of all his good promise, which he spoke by Moses his servant" (I Kings 8:56). Solomon described the nation's current condition as rest that God had promised and provided to His people. The king then looked to a future he hoped would be marked by obedience to God (see I Kings 8:54-61) and acknowledged God's global purposes in fulfilling His promises for His chosen people: "that all the peoples of the earth may know that the LORD is God; there is no other" (I Kings 8:60).

Underline the phrase in both verses that describes the standard of accuracy with which God fulfilled His promises to His chosen people.

"Not one word of all the good promises that the LORD had made to the house of Israel had failed; all came to pass." *Joshua 21:45*

"Blessed be the LORD who has given rest to his people Israel, according to all that he promised. Not one word has failed of all his good promise, which he spoke by Moses his servant." *1 Kings 8:56*

There wasn't one instance when Joshua or Solomon could look back and say, "Well, that didn't turn out quite the way God said it would." History had unfolded exactly the way God declared it would. The people had tested God's promises, and not one word had failed.

Testing God's Promises

When we think about testing God's promises, we might fall into the error of picturing ourselves as lab technicians overseeing grand experiments in which we have God's Word under a microscope. That's the wrong picture. Our lives are the lab. Our lives are proof of the Word of God. There is a massive experiment under way in which all of us are participating. Is God's Word true? Does it bear itself out in our lives?

Our lives are proof of the Word of God.

In its totality God's Word is a bunch of promises and consequences. God said in Deuteronomy 11:26-28, "See, I am setting before you today a blessing and a curse: the blessing, if you obey the commandments of the LORD your God, … and the curse, if you do not obey the commandments of the LORD your God." One way or another we prove the Word of God. If you obey, you will be blessed.

Your life is proof of that promise. If you disobey, you will be judged. Your life is proof of this consequence.

Try to identify at least one experience in your life that tested each of the following kinds of promises God has given in His Word.

Promises of protection (see Ps. 23; 37:25; 1 Pet. 5:7):

Promises of provision (see Ps. 84:11; Rom. 8:32; Phil. 4:19):

Promises of perseverance (see Isa. 30:18; 40:31; Rom. 8:37-39):

At this point you may be thinking, *James, you're saying God invites us to test His promises, but didn't Jesus tell Satan, "You shall not put the Lord your God to the test" (Matt. 4:7)?* Good question, and I'm glad for the chance to clarify. Jesus' warning not to put God to the test means two things.

1. Don't act foolishly and expect God to bail you out. In Matthew 4 Satan was tempting Jesus to jump from the pinnacle of the temple to see whether God would send angels to catch Him. Sounds like something junior-high boys might do rather than the Son of God. If Jesus had fallen for that ploy, not only would He have made a rash move, but He would have also revealed doubt about His own identity. The dare from the Devil was "If you are the Son of God ..." Jesus didn't have to prove something He already knew.

Some people take one of God's promises and push it to the limit. Take, for instance, His promise to meet our needs in Philippians 4:19: "My God will supply every need of yours according to his riches in glory in Christ Jesus." God promises that, as a believer, you will never lack the basic provisions of life—food, shelter, and clothing. One way or another God will take care of those. Some people twist His promise and say, "Well, then, let's sell the house. Let's give away all our money. Torch the car, and let's go sit in a field. Take care of me *now*, God!" Not testing God means not to act foolishly and then expect God to bail you out.

God promises that, as a believer, you will never lack the basic provisions of life.

2. Don't act willfully and provoke God to judge you for rebellion and ungratefulness. When Jesus responded to Satan in Matthew 4, he was quoting Deuteronomy 6:16: "You shall not put the LORD your God to the test, as you tested him at Massah." Massah, which means *testing*, was a place where the Israelites camped (see Ex. 17) after God had brought them out of Egypt, out of slavery, and out of harm's way. Although He fed them every day with bread from heaven, one day the group woke up and went ballistic because there was a temporary water shortage. Moses was afraid for his life as the people turned against God.

Here's a warning: don't *ever* do that. Don't put God to the threat test. Don't disregard every good thing He has done for you, turn rebellious and ungrateful, and whine, "But I *have* to have this, God. If You don't fix this situation, You're not God. You don't care about me." Don't put it all on the line over one thing and demand that God work right now. When we try this, we are not depending on God so much as we are trying to demonstrate just how much influence we have with Him. Ordering God around is not going to turn out well for us. Even if He graciously intervenes, as He did with the Israelites at Massah, we will find it almost impossible to be grateful.

God doesn't want us to put Him to the test—His character, His compassion, His purposes—but he wants us to test His promises. Why? Because He wants us to know for certain—from experience—that what He promises is true. When we learn that lesson, we are better able to walk in faith.

> **Identify a trial or problem you are experiencing that would allow you to test God's promises.**

> **Spend time in prayer, thanking God for the promises that have proved true in your life. Praise Him as the great Promise Keeper whose Word stands up to anything we face in life. Ask Him to help you step out in faith on the promises He has given for any trials or problems you are experiencing.**

> **Practice saying this week's memory verses, 2 Peter 1:3-4.**

Don't put God to the threat test.

Day 4

GOD'S PROMISES ARE ACTIVATED BY FAITH

Today's Scripture Focus

"He did not do many mighty works there, because of their unbelief."
Matthew 13:58

"You desire and do not have, so you murder. You covet and cannot obtain,
so you fight and quarrel. You do not have, because you do not ask.
You ask and do not receive, because you ask wrongly,
to spend it on your passions." *James 4:2-3*

Sometimes we think things would be different if Jesus were still here on earth. What do you really think would happen if Jesus showed up in your neighborhood? It's easy to think, *If Jesus were here, things would be different. Miracles would happen. People would be changed. More people would be willing to believe in Him.* Matthew 13:58 tells us, "Not necessarily."

The Obstacle of Unbelief

Jesus had come back home to Nazareth, His base for ministry when He was in the north of Israel. In the previous chapter Jesus was elsewhere teaching and healing when His mother and brothers showed up to intervene. We don't know what they planned to tell Jesus, but it's probably safe to say Mary was concerned for her son, and His brothers just wanted to tell Him something like "What are You thinking?" In any case Jesus let them know that His standard for prioritizing relationships in His life was as follows: "Whoever does the will of my Father in heaven is my brother and sister and mother" (Matt. 12:50). He wasn't rejecting them; He was simply clarifying their relationship.

When Jesus returned to Nazareth, He tried to continue His ministry of teaching, but the locals, who thought they knew Him, didn't believe He could be what He seemed. In Matthew 13:54-56 they basically passed around the high-school yearbook and said, "See? This is Mary's Son. Remember? Here are all of His brothers and sisters. We know Him. Who does He think he is?" Verse 57 expresses it this way: "They took offense at him." Familiarity bred contempt. Their question was "Where did this man get this wisdom and these mighty works?" (v. 54). But they weren't looking for an answer; they were asking as a way

> The locals, who thought they knew Jesus, didn't believe He could be what He seemed.

of saying they rejected Him. Jesus didn't argue with them. He simply pointed out, "A prophet is not without honor except in his hometown and in his own household" (v. 57). At that point Matthew added the sad note that Jesus "did not do many mighty works there, because of their unbelief" (v. 58). Though Jesus' family and neighbors already knew about Jesus' teaching and mighty works, they were unwilling to believe.

Check any works you or others in your church have asked God to do, but He has not acted.

☐ Lord, why don't You do more in and through our church?
☐ You do so many good things for my friend. Why don't You bless me that way?
☐ Why won't You heal my loved one's illness?
☐ Other:

Many of us are familiar with Jesus and what He can do. Not nearly as many of us can report that God's promises are coming true in our lives. Why is this? Just like the people of Nazareth, we've got a problem with unbelief. Unbelief is an obstacle in a Christian's spiritual walk. God's promises are activated by faith.

Maybe you know all about a weight-loss plan. You might be able to list the foods, the calories, and the exercise plan, but you won't lose weight unless you follow the plan. You can be familiar with a piece of music, but it's not yours until you play it. A doctor's prescription can match your illness perfectly, but until you swallow the medicine, it's not going to make any difference in your health.

You've got to take God's promises by faith.

You've got to take God's promises by faith. Only then will you experience for yourself why they have satisfied generations of faithful men and women who have trusted God's Word.

Check the areas of your life in which you need to exercise faith in God's promises.

☐ Marriage   ☐ Family
☐ Physical or emotional illness   ☐ Career
☐ Spiritual growth   ☐ Relationships
☐ Witnessing to others   ☐ Grief
☐ Ministering to others   ☐ Depression
☐ Other:

Activating Your Faith

God's promises are activated by faith. Faith is not passive; it's an action word. If you say, "I'm waiting for God to act. Maybe He will work; maybe He won't," you are acting like a sick guy who needs to get better but won't go to the doctor. Or like a single woman who is looking for a husband but never goes to the single-adult group at church. Or people who are filled with worry and want to have hope but never read the Bible. They might carry it and respect it and defend it, but they're not drinking from the Word of life like someone thirsting in a desert. They're not living in it and believing God's promises for their needs.

James wrote, "You desire and do not have, so you murder. You covet and cannot obtain, so you fight and quarrel. You do not have, because you do not ask. You ask and do not receive, because you ask wrongly, to spend it on your passions" (Jas. 4:2-3). If you aren't seeing God work in your situation, get your heart around some of His exceedingly great and precious promises. Hold on to what He has said in His Word. If you have God's promises hidden in your heart, His words will fill your life with faith.

Read the story of Naaman in 2 Kings 5:1-14 and answer these questions.

Why was Naaman at first unwilling to follow Elisha's instructions?

What does this story tell us about placing faith in God's word?

Identify an area of your life in which you have not been willing to search for God's promise and act in faith on it.

Here are three ways we can actively rely on God's promises.

See the promises. Bible studies can teach you a lot about God's Word, but no Bible study can replace your personal reading of God's Word. Persistently and consistently read the Bible. Examine it closely and apply it rigorously. There's something unforgettable about discovering one of God's promises on your own as the Holy Spirit opens your eyes. It's like a light going on.

> If you have God's promises hidden in your heart, His words will fill your life with faith.

Part of seeing a Bible promise is to understand it in context. Some promises are unique to particular situations and individuals. Others are universal, applying to all people at all times.

Read the following verses and indicate whether they are unique or universal.

Judges 13:3-5	☐ Unique	☐ Universal
Psalm 23:4	☐ Unique	☐ Universal
Isaiah 43:2	☐ Unique	☐ Universal
Luke 1:31	☐ Unique	☐ Universal

The promises God made, for example, to Samson's parents and to Mary applied only to their circumstances. However, you can take hold of the promises God has universally guaranteed to all of His children, asking God to open your eyes to their universal truth as well as their particular relevance for your life.

Read Isaiah 43:2.

> "When you pass through the waters, I will be with you;
> and through the rivers, they shall not overwhelm you;
> when you walk through fire you shall not be burned,
> and the flame shall not consume you."

In what circumstances would you apply this verse to your life?

Savor the promises. If you want to experience God's promises for yourself, you've got to feed on them with your mind. Learn to treasure them in your heart. Allow them to nourish your soul. The law that the wise person in Psalm 1 meditates on day and night is flavored with God's promises. Tasting and seeing that the Lord is good also has a lot to do with living with His promises:

> "Oh, taste and see that the LORD is good!
> Blessed is the man who takes refuge in him!" *Psalm 34:8*

Savoring God's promises involves rolling them over and through your mind as you would savor the taste of delicious food in your mouth. As you pray a scriptural promise, expect it and believe it as already accomplished. Thank God in faith that it is already happening. I often pray a promise like this: "Even though it's not visual to me, God, by faith I believe Your Word. I believe You are

As you pray a scriptural promise, expect it and believe it as already accomplished.

at work today bringing this about. You said You're with me, so I believe it. I'm expecting You to make a way even though I can't see it up ahead." Because they are certain, God's promises give you permission to visualize the done deal.

Read Psalm 27:13.

> "I believe that I shall look upon the goodness of the LORD
> in the land of the living!"

After meditating on this verse, identify what specific goodness you long to see in the land of the living.

Share the promises. As you discover promises for your trials or needs, share them with others. Don't worry about appearing to be a spiritual giant. Give God the credit and invite others to share in the benefits of God's promises. Also report to others how God is fulfilling His promises in your life. Get excited when other people see, savor, and share God's promises.

Report to others how God is fulfilling His promises in your life.

Read Romans 10:9.

> "If you confess with your mouth that Jesus is Lord and believe in your
> heart that God raised him from the dead, you will be saved."

Who in your life needs to hear that promise today?

Pray for opportunities to share the salvation of Jesus with the person(s) you named. Ask God for opportunities to share His promises with others.

Write this week's memory verses, 2 Peter 1:3-4, here from memory.

GOD'S PROMISES ARE EXPERIENCED IN JESUS CHRIST

Today's Scripture Focus

"All the promises of God find their Yes in him. That is why it is through him that we utter our Amen to God for his glory." *2 Corinthians 1:20*

You are standing outside your favorite store when someone who knows you very well hands you an envelope and says, "I've decided to bless you today. I know you and what you want and need. In this envelope is a lengthy list of everything in this store that I'm prepared to give you. You can't afford any of this yourself, but I'm offering it all to you. Ask for anything on the list, and I'll say yes."

There are two actions you can take right after you say, "Thank you very much!" You can tear open the envelope and use it as a shopping list, or you can take your amazing friend into the store with you and walk up and down the aisles, carrying the unopened envelope as you continually ask, "Can I have this? Can I have that?" Because you would be guessing, sometimes the answer would be "Yes, that's on the list." But often the answer would be "No, that's not on the list."

So why not tear open the envelope and look at the list?

Second Corinthians 1:20, today's Scripture focus, begins, "All the promises of God find their Yes in him," that is, in Jesus. We can stumble through our lives wondering whether God would grant us what we want and need, but the reality is that these things are already on the list.

Read Ephesians 1:3 and 2 Peter 1:3.

"Blessed be the God and Father of our Lord Jesus Christ, who has blessed us in Christ with every spiritual blessing in the heavenly places." *Ephesians 1:3*

"His divine power has granted to us all things that pertain to life and godliness, through the knowledge of him who called us to his own glory and excellence." *2 Peter 1:3*

Check the things God has already promised us.

- ☐ Material wealth
- ☐ Good health
- ☐ Resources for godly living
- ☐ Spiritual blessings
- ☐ An earthly kingdom
- ☐ Life in Christ

Because we have life in Christ, God has promised to supply every spiritual blessing and everything we need for godly living. Every promise we will savor in this study and every promise you discover in God's Word will be experienced in, guaranteed by, and delivered through Jesus Christ. God's promises are wrapped up in Jesus Christ. Romans 11:36 says of Him, "From him and through him and to him are all things." Jesus Christ is the promise of God.

Jesus Christ is the promise of God.

Christ in You

This may come as a shock to you, but it is impossible for you to live the Christian life. You can't do it on your own. The Christian life isn't something you do. The Christian life is "Christ in you, the hope of glory" (Col. 1:27).

When you accepted Christ as your Savior and Lord, you died. "I have been crucified with Christ," Galatians 2:20 teaches. "It is no longer I who live, but Christ who lives in me. And the life I now live in the flesh I live by faith in the Son of God, who loved me and gave himself for me." Jesus is your life. It's not trying to please the Lord or impress Him or imitate Him. The Christian life is all about yielding to the living presence of Christ in you by His Spirit.

Mark the point on the scale that represents your ability to allow Christ to live His life through you.

●————————————————————————————————●

Doing and performing   **Yielding to Christ's living presence in me**

If the Christian life for you is acting like Jesus, that's just religion. Performing and trying to be a Christian gets stale, ritualistic, and exhausting after a while. Pretty soon we throw everything up in the air and say, "I can't do all this!" Correct. He never said we could. Instead, *He* is the Christian life.

You may be wondering what it looks like in the Christian life to let Jesus live through you: *How can I let Jesus do it when the Bible tells me to obey so many commands?* Let's look at 1 Thessalonians 5:16-22 to get a picture of our dilemma:

"Rejoice always, pray without ceasing, give thanks in all circumstances;
for this is the will of God in Christ Jesus for you. Do not quench
the Spirit. Do not despise prophecies, but test everything;
hold fast what is good. Abstain from every form of evil."

At first blush this passage looks like a grocery list of all the stuff we have to do in the Christian life. Rejoice always. Pray without ceasing. Give thanks in all circumstances. Like a juggler trying to keep all of the balls in the air, maybe we just need to get more skillful in the Christian life, add more disciplines, get more dedicated, and increase our capacity for doing even more. But that's not it at all. Look at the next two verses:

"May the God of peace himself sanctify you completely,
and may your whole spirit and soul and body be kept
blameless at the coming of our Lord Jesus Christ. He who
calls you is faithful; he will surely do it" (vv. 23-24).

Jesus doesn't just call us to it. He does it. We can't sanctify ourselves. It is Jesus who makes us "partakers of the divine nature" (2 Pet. 1:4). We can't walk and work by faith. "It is God who works in you, both to will and to work for his good pleasure" (Phil. 2:13). Once again, Jesus Christ *is* the Christian life. For everything you can't do, He will surely do it.

What is a specific problem or situation that has you feeling helpless and clueless about what to do?

Maybe your problem is a seeming inability to live in the power and wisdom of Christ. Confess any attempts you have made to fix things in your own power. Then ask Jesus to help you withstand temptation, endure a trial, be faithful to persevere, and yield to His indwelling presence.

Every Promise Is Yours

What we have observed about life in Christ gives us a foundation for understanding how He grants us the promises in God's Word. Just as we can't make ourselves godly or obedient in the Christian life, we can't access the promises of God on our own. You see, Jesus doesn't give us the promises. He gives us Himself. When we receive Him, we receive every promise in Scripture.

When we receive
Jesus, we receive
every promise in
Scripture.

Let's look at each of the five promises we are going to study in weeks 2–6 and discover their source in Jesus Christ.

1. I will not fear; God is always with me. Specifically, it's Jesus who is with us: "I am with you always, to the end of the age" (Matt. 28:20). Christ's presence in our lives takes away fear.

2. I will not doubt; God is always in control. Hebrews 1:3 says Jesus "upholds the universe by the word of his power." As the instrument of God's sovereignty, Jesus holds the whole world in His hands. Christ's sovereignty gives us assurance and calmness in the face of doubts.

3. I will not despair; God is always good. Jesus, who said, "I am the good shepherd" (John 10:11), protects and takes care of His sheep. Christ's goodness renews us when we are weighed down by despair.

4. I will not falter; God is always watching. Colossians 1:15-17 illustrates Jesus' attentive interest in all He has created. Romans 8:34 pictures Him at the right hand of God interceding for us. When Jesus was on earth, each person who met Him received exactly what they needed under His compassionate attention. Christ's strength keeps us from faltering.

5. I will not fail; God is always victorious. Scripture repeatedly tells us Jesus Christ is always victorious. In John 16:33 He asserted, "In the world you will have tribulation. But take heart; I have overcome the world." Someday the clouds will break open, and He will return as King of kings and Lord of lords. Christ's present and future victory assures us we will not fail.

Christ's present and future victory assures us we will not fail.

> **Underline the Scripture in points 1–5 above that speaks to your greatest need or concern at this time in your life.**

> **Recite your memory verses for this week, 2 Peter 1:3-4, as a prayer. Thank Jesus that through Him you have become a partaker of the divine nature and that every promise of God is yes in Him.**

Week 2

I WILL NOT FEAR
GOD IS ALWAYS WITH ME

This Week's Promise

I WILL NOT FEAR; GOD IS ALWAYS WITH ME.

I will not doubt; God is always in control.

I will not despair; God is always good.

I will not falter; God is always watching.

I will not fail; God is always victorious.

This Week's Memory Verse

"Be strong and courageous. Do not fear or be in dread of them, for it is the LORD your God who goes with you. He will not leave you or forsake you."

Deuteronomy 31:6

Divine Problem Solving

Stretching across 277 miles, the Grand Canyon ranges from a half mile to 18 miles wide and comprises one million acres of land. The area totals 1.2 million acres, and the average depth of the canyon is almost 1 mile. It is the home to 75 species of mammals, 50 reptiles, 75 kinds of fish, and 300 species of birds. My father brought our family to the Grand Canyon when I was growing up. He wanted to instill in his children an appreciation for the creative genius of Almighty God.

Perhaps more than any other natural setting, the Grand Canyon impresses us with the sheer scale of God's creation. Psalm 104:8 says,

> "The mountains rose, the valleys sank down
> to the place that you appointed for them."

This verse pictures the Creator carving out deep gullies, heaping up enormous mountains, and sculpting rocky crags according to His grand design—as easily as we would construct a sand castle on the beach. Such a picture gives us some perspective on the confidence with which God approaches our problems when we cry out to Him for help. Our trials appear huge to us, but God looks at them and says, "Behold, I am the LORD, the God of all flesh. Is anything too hard for me?" (Jer. 32:27).

God has given us His promises as tools for solving our problems in life. Too often when we are confronted with a challenge or difficulty, our first response is to ask, "How can I figure out a way around or through this problem?" But when we get steeped in God's Word, our first question becomes "How many of God's promises directly apply to this problem?" Our problems might confound us, but they are *never* a surprise to God. He knows what's coming, and the promises He has provided in His Word can prepare us ahead of time for whatever we might face.

This week we will examine one of the most common problems in life—fear. When fear arises, you can open God's Word and find promises that will cut that fear down to size.

GROUP EXPERIENCE

On the Same Page

1. Share your experiences with recent do-it-yourself home projects and describe the results.

2. Which word or phrase most accurately describes your toolbox?
   • Useless   • Complete—all of the right tools   • Just the essentials
   • I have to borrow what I need from my neighbor.
   How important is having the right tools for the job?

3. Share an experience from your life illustrating that God's promises are like tools we can use to fix or solve our problems.

Preparation and Review

1. Memorizing God's Word allows us to develop an internal toolbox of God's promises that immediately come to mind when we face a problem. Ask a volunteer to recite last week's memory verses.

2. Together read aloud this week's memory verse on page 34.

3. What did you learn last week about the role God's promises play in a walk of faith?

DVD Session 2 Viewer Guide

Promise number 1 deals with problem number 1: I will not _____.

Before we can appreciate what the _____ solves, we need to know what the _____ is.

Fear just _____.

One of the most common exhortations from God's messengers is "_____ _____" or "Do _____ _____."

Fear is the complete state of _____-God.

Fear is always _____.

The antidote for fear is the promise "_____ is with me."

Promise 1: I will not _fear_ ; _God_ is with me.

God is not with _____.

1. God is not with the _____ (see Ps. 138:6).
2. God is not with the _____ (see Jas. 4:4).
3. God is not with the _____ (see Isa. 1:5).
4. God is not with those who harbor _____ (see Ps. 66:18).

If God already gave you His _____, will He not give you something _____ if you ask Him (see Rom. 8:32)?

_____ _____ is praying for us (see Rom. 8:34).

If you put your whole _____ on God's promise, it holds you up (see Heb. 13:5-6).

I will not fear; God is with me _____ (see Deut. 31:6).

Responding to the DVD Teaching

1. Psalm 34:18 says,

"The LORD is near to the brokenhearted
and saves the crushed in spirit."

How have you seen God draw near to you during hard times?

2. What is the difference between fear knocking on the door and fear moving in for an extended stay? What's wrong with the picture of God and fear living in the same house?

3. What have you found doesn't work when dealing with fear?

4. How do you know you can confidently say, "God is with me"?

5. What are some specific fears in your life that we can pray about this week?

Read week 2 and complete the activities before the next group experience. Read and recite this week's memory verse, Deuteronomy 31:6, at least once each day this week.

This video session is available for download at *www.lifeway.com/alwaystrue.*

Day 1
WHAT ARE YOU AFRAID OF?

Today's Scripture Focus

"Even though I walk through the valley of the shadow of death,
I will fear no evil,
for you are with me;
your rod and your staff,
they comfort me."
Psalm 23:4

Psalm 23:4 is one of the most familiar thoughts in all of Scripture. And yet we don't usually think of that passage as a promise. We turn to it for comfort when dealing with the deaths of others, but we often fail to see that every verse in Psalm 23 contains one or more promises about living.

As you read Psalm 23, underline the promises you find. I have completed verse 1 for you.

"<u>The LORD is my shepherd</u>; I shall not want.
He makes me lie down in green pastures.
He leads me beside still waters.
He restores my soul.
He leads me in paths of righteousness for his name's sake.
Even though I walk through the valley of the shadow of death,
I will fear no evil,
for you are with me;
your rod and your staff,
they comfort me.
You prepare a table before me
in the presence of my enemies;
you anoint my head with oil;
my cup overflows.
Surely goodness and mercy shall follow me
all the days of my life,
and I shall dwell in the house of the LORD forever."

List some of the fears the psalmist names or suggests.

Psalm 23 identifies not only one or more of God's promises but also one or more things that might cause fear to come knocking on our door—basic needs, stress, assaults by an enemy, evil, and death itself. When we read or hear the words "Even though I walk through the valley of the shadow of death" (v. 4), we tend to think we might make an occasional, temporary visit to the neighborhood of death, after which we will quickly get back to the plains of life or the mountaintops of spiritual good times. But the verse actually means "Even though I live in the valley of the shadow of death." When are we *not* living under the shadow of death? Life this side of eternity is a journey through that valley. Sometimes we feel the shadows are deeper, but they are always there. And an awareness of the valley is always an opportunity for fear to come knocking. That's why fear is a problem that must be confronted by a continual awareness that God is in the valley with us as our Shepherd every single moment.

The first verse of the psalm, "The Lord is my shepherd," is not a bad way to state our promise for this week, "God is with me." When David wrote, "I will fear no evil, for you are with me" (v. 4), he was personalizing and putting into a particular context the specific promise and problem we are addressing this week: I will not fear; God is always with me.

Naming Your Fears

The Bible recognizes that one of our greatest problems in life is fear. We can dress fear up in all kinds of costumes or drive it undercover. But it is never very far away from any of us.

What are your three biggest fears in life right now? How do they affect you?

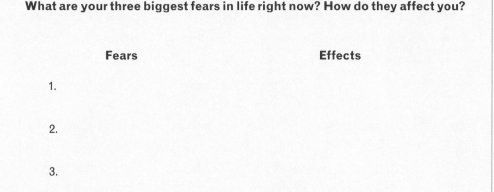

	Fears	Effects
1.		
2.		
3.		

We fear the future.

In general, we fear the future. No one is afraid of the past. The past creates other problems, like regrets and consequences. And no one is really afraid of the present. We might be upset about it, but we don't fear it because we know it. But we fear the future because it is unknown. Anxiety dreads the future.

When we think about the future, we fear loss and pain.

- We are afraid of losing people. Will my husband always love me? Will this friendship last? Will my kids walk with the Lord or go their own way?

- We dread losing possessions. I'm barely able to make ends meet; will I be able to keep my house? Will there be money for my kids to go to college?

- We are anxious over losing our position. I've worked hard; I have an opportunity. Will I lose it? I'm in over my head; will they find out?

- We recoil from physical pain. How can I cope with this chronic condition? Will this pain ever get better?

- We are terrified about emotional pain. Somebody's not happy with me. They don't want me anymore.

- We fear failure. I'm not happy with myself. I could have. I should have. I would have. But I didn't. I'm not good enough. I failed.

Go back and check the fears you share in the previous list.

Defining Fear

Fear is a universal problem. It hits us like a wave, threatening to swallow us in its undertow. Scripture identifies the overwhelming emotion of fear almost a thousand times. The word *fear* is used 441 times; *afraid*, 167 times; *tremble*, 101 times; and *terror* or *terrified*, 121 times. The words *dread*, *frighten*, and *faint* are also repeatedly used throughout Scripture.

Many biblical characters—even those we think of as spiritual giants—had to face enormous fears. Abraham was afraid he would never have a male heir. Moses was initially afraid to accept God's call to lead the Hebrews out of Egypt. The Israelites were terrified as the Egyptians bore down on them and they faced the barrier of the Red Sea. David feared for his life many times when Saul pursued him. And you probably recall the way the disciples reacted when the soldiers came and arrested Jesus in the garden of Gethsemane.

Will you receive fear into your heart and mind, or will you listen to God's promises?

Your fears may or may not be as daunting as those of these biblical characters. But the question for you is the same one they had to answer: Will you receive fear into your heart and mind, or will you listen to God's promises?

How do you deal with the fears you have identified?

- ☐ Invite them in for a visit
- ☐ Seek and believe God's promises
- ☐ Deny my fears; try not to think about them
- ☐ Panic
- ☐ Other:

Some emotional responses have their place. Take anger. You could be angry about injustice or unrighteousness. That kind of righteous anger is a good thing. It drives positive action. This is exactly the kind of anger that filled Jesus as He strode through the temple courts, overturning the counters of the money changers and cleaning up His Father's house (see Matt. 21:12-13).

Grief is also acceptable for a season. When a loved one dies or you go through any profound loss, you need time to work through it. There is a healthy and necessary adjustment to the sudden absence of someone or something important. Grief has a purpose. Fear never does. The Bible tells us it is wrong to live in a state of fear. In the Old Testament God repeatedly instructed people not to be afraid but to trust in Him (see Gen. 15:1; 21:17; Ex. 14:13). And in the New Testament Paul instructed Christians, "You did not receive the spirit of slavery to fall back into fear" (Rom. 8:15) and "God gave us a spirit not of fear but of power and love and self-control" (2 Tim. 1:7).

Some sins grab you and imprison you. Fear does that. Dread locks you in a small, dark room and sinks its clammy claws into your spirit. Terror is tough to shake. Once you've given it a place in your heart, it becomes an addictive drug you can't live without. The problem isn't when fear stops by for a visit. The problem is when you open the front door and invite it in: "Fear! Welcome back! I've been waiting for you! Your room is ready down the hall." When you receive fear into your mind, heart, and life and nourish it like a friend, that's a problem.

Fear can be defined as the complete state of anti-God. God is seldom farther from you than when your heart is filled with fear. Fear is completely relying on your own resources and suddenly realizing they aren't nearly enough to sustain you. Fear has no place in the life of a Christian. A fearful response—an anxious, frightened reaction—is never healthy, and it's never from God.

> **Fear can be defined as the complete state of anti-God.**

In light of this definition of fear, what needs to change in the way you are handling your fears?

When we look at a threat and forget to keep God's promises in mind, that enemy appears to take on added power or danger. Fear always makes the problem or the enemy larger than it really is. The armies of Israel looked at Goliath and saw an enemy too strong and too big to defeat (see 1 Sam. 17). By comparing the giant to themselves rather than comparing him to God, they allowed their fears to add to his stature and power. On the other hand, David looked at Goliath and saw a target too big to miss! His confidence in God made him read the evidence in a different way than the others did.

On almost any day we can look at "evidence" in our lives that suggests God isn't in control and we shouldn't hope in Him. Fear whispers, "God is not with you," using limited and distorted evidence to make its case. But as soon as we let God back into the picture, He dwarfs everything else. His presence reveals false evidence for what it is.

If what we fear gets no power from God, where does the power of fear come from?

Look at the three fears you listed on page 39. How do they tempt you with false evidence?

Read today's Scripture focus, Psalm 23:4, on page 38. How does this promise refute the false evidence of your fears?

If you are a believer, God is not only with you but also in you. Look at these verses: "Do you not know that you are God's temple and that God's Spirit dwells in you? If anyone destroys God's temple, God will destroy him. For God's temple is holy, and you are that temple" (1 Cor. 3:16-17). "Do you not know that your body is a temple of the Holy Spirit within you, whom you have from God? You are not your own" (1 Cor. 6:19). You are God's dwelling place, a temple devoted to worshiping and obeying God. Fear has no place here. The only explanation for its presence is that you are giving it permission to roam through the premises.

Pray and ask God to help you overcome fear as you believe His promises. Tell Him you want your temple to be a clean vessel for His use.

Day 2
THE SOLUTION TO THE FEAR PROBLEM

Today's Scripture Focus

"He has said, 'I will never leave you nor forsake you.'
So we can confidently say, 'The Lord is my helper;
I will not fear; what can man do to me?' "

Hebrews 13:5-6

In today's Scripture focus the writer of Hebrews fought fear by quoting promises of God that were already on the record. The words of Hebrews 13:5, "I will never leave you nor forsake you," echo God's promise to Joshua in Joshua 1:5: "No man shall be able to stand before you all the days of your life. Just as I was with Moses, so I will be with you. I will not leave you or forsake you." Under the inspiration of the Holy Spirit, the writer of Hebrews took an individual promise given to Joshua and made it applicable to all of us.

The second quoted promise in Hebrews 13:5-6 is from Psalm 118:6:

"The Lord is on my side; I will not fear.
What can man do to me?"

If the Lord is with us on one side of the teeter-totter, it doesn't matter who, how many, or what else is on the other side. Our side isn't going to move.

Think about some of your fears. How do they tempt you to feel that God has forsaken you at times?

> No matter what the fear, God will never leave us or forsake us.

Everlasting Love

Try to grasp the reality that no matter what the fear, God will never leave us or forsake us. Why is He willing to be on our side? It certainly isn't because He needs us. It's because He loves us.

Even when we go through hard times and experience God's discipline, He never forsakes us. God's chosen people, Israel, experienced the Father's love and blessing like no other nation in history. Yet they turned their back on God, indulging in immorality and idolatry. After years of rebellion and apostasy, the nation came under God's judgment in 587 B.C. and was defeated by the Babylonians. Nevertheless, even though they were in captivity, they remained the object of God's undying love: "I have loved you with an everlasting love" (Jer. 31:3), God reminded the people through the prophet Jeremiah.

God regards us the same way. It was because of His great love that He sent His Son to redeem sinful, rebellious humanity. Those of us who know Jesus enjoy a special relationship of love that is intimate and eternal. The apostle John explained, "God is love. In this the love of God was made manifest among us, that God sent his only Son into the world, so that we might live through him. In this is love, not that we have loved God but that he loved us and sent his Son to be the propitiation for our sins" (I John 4:8-10).

Through our relationship with Christ, we can know God is with us because He wants to be with those He loves. Our experience of the reality and fear-busting power of His presence depends on our accepting His love and responding to it with all the love we have to give.

> **If you haven't accepted the gift of Jesus' payment for your sin, you won't have access to His resources for dealing with fear or any other problem in your life. He loved you so much that He died to pay for your sin, and He wants to have an intimate relationship with you that will never end. Confess your sin to Him and place your trust in His saving power. If you do that, He will never leave you or forsake you.**

A Trust Walk

Once you are convinced of God's love—an undying love that will never abandon you—you are equipped to trust Him. The specific tool you use to deal with fear is faith. If someone who is scared to death says, "God is with me; I will not fear," the statement will not make any difference in their situation. If you have no trust in the truth of these words, they won't help you. You have to declare these words, believe these words, and then behave based on these words. Why? Because they are based on the character of God. He is faithful, and you can place your trust in what He has promised.

The specific tool you use to deal with fear is faith.

Fear tries to distract us from trusting. On the other hand, the deliberate choice to trust God on our part almost immediately begins to evict fear.

Mark the continuum to indicate the degree to which you are trusting God with your fears.

●────────────────────────────────────●

Trembling with fear   Gutting it out   No fear!

Read Psalm 9:10; Psalm 40:4; Isaiah 12:2. How do these verses speak to your struggle with fear today?

God with Us

God is with you. Isn't that typical of what a pastor would say? I figured you might be thinking that. *God is with you, Brother. And you too, Sister.* But what does that really mean? Exactly how does that work?

When I developed this teaching, Kathy and I were going through a very difficult season involving one of our kids. Kathy and I did everything we could as parents—and it wasn't enough. There was a gap of helplessness, fear, and even anger that drove home the point that we are not ultimately in control (a hard thing to face as a parent). As we came to the end of our resources, ideas, and strength, Kathy and I had to put everything on the line and believe that the promise of God's unchanging presence is true. But even more importantly, God is staking His reputation on this promise. He makes it very personal: " 'I will never leave you nor forsake you.' So we can confidently say, 'The Lord is my helper; I will not fear; what can man do to me?' "(Heb. 13:5-6). We discovered this fact: you can put your whole weight on this promise, and it holds you up. It sustains you. Through every intense, heart-wrenching moment of this trial, God's presence became increasingly real.

Fear must be replaced by trust. Fear looks at the real or imaginary thing that is provoking those feelings. Trust deliberately looks to God, concentrates on God's Word, knows the promises God has provided, and applies them to the situation.

Fear must be replaced by trust.

Recall one of the fears you listed in day 1 (p. 39). In what specific ways are you placing your trust in God in regard to this fear? Check all that apply.

☐ Praying
☐ Reading the promises of God's Word
☐ Applying God's promises to your situation
☐ Believing God will never leave you or forsake you
☐ Other:

Practice reciting this week's memory verse, Deuteronomy 31:6.

Day 3

GOD'S PRESENCE

Today's Scripture Focus

"Am I a God at hand, declares the LORD, and not a God far away?
Can a man hide himself in secret places so that I cannot see him?
declares the LORD. Do I not fill heaven and earth? declares the LORD."

Jeremiah 23:23-24

"Where shall I go from your Spirit?
Or where shall I flee from your presence?
If I ascend to heaven, you are there!
If I make my bed in Sheol, you are there!
If I take the wings of the morning
and dwell in the uttermost parts of the sea,
even there your hand shall lead me,
and your right hand shall hold me."

Psalm 139:7-10

This week we've been examining the promise "God is always with me" as the antidote to fear. As today's Scripture focus teaches, God is everywhere in His creation. He is immediately and continually accessible in any and every place. Yes, God is everywhere; therefore, He is where we are. In the truest sense, God is not in *our* presence; we are in *His* presence. Distance makes no difference to God.

Our connection with God is intimate and immediate.

At the same time, we need to understand that "God is always with me" includes more than the fact of His omnipresence. If we are believers in Jesus Christ, God is with us *individually*. When we became His children, He came to live in each of us personally, and each of us dwells in Him: "Whoever confesses that Jesus is the Son of God, God abides in him, and he in God. So we have come to know and to believe the love that God has for us. God is love, and whoever abides in love abides in God, and God abides in him" (1 John 4:15-16). Because Christ lives in us, God is with Christians in a way that is different from what an unbeliever can experience. Our connection with God is intimate and immediate.

How has Christ's indwelling presence helped you face hard times in the past?

Christ's presence in us eliminates fear: "There is no fear in love, but perfect love casts out fear. For fear has to do with punishment, and whoever fears has not been perfected in love" (1 John 4:18). The more we give ourselves to knowing and experiencing the reality of God's presence in our lives and the love He has for us, the less fear will be able to control us.

Always Near

In Jeremiah 23:24 God asks, "Can a man hide himself in secret places so that I cannot see him?" Because God is everywhere, He is always near.

The first hint that something had gone terribly wrong in the world came when someone tried to hide from God. After Adam and Eve sinned, they tried to hide from God's presence (see Gen. 3:8). When God asked where they were, He wasn't doing it because He didn't know. He did it because He wanted Adam and Eve to acknowledge their situation. You see, what we think is hiding, God knows is lost and clueless. Adam had to confess, "I was afraid" (Gen. 3:10). When Adam explained his fear of being seen naked, he actually revealed the terror of being exposed, which goes beyond nakedness. Adam knew he had violated God's command and wouldn't be able to hide that fact when he encountered God, so he tried to hide himself instead.

How have your current fears caused you to move toward God or to hide from Him?

When you face hard times, it sometimes feels that God backs away from you. But the reality is that God is right there with you in your trial. When you're going through hardship or when you're heavyhearted and burdened, God rolls up His sleeves and moves toward you in a way that's unlike any other time. It doesn't matter whether you see Him working. His approach may not cause you to feel any different. But it's the truth: the harder the days get, the closer God leans in so that you can hear His voice. Psalm 34:18 says,

> "The LORD is near to the brokenhearted
> and saves the crushed in spirit."

The harder the days get, the closer God leans in so that you can hear His voice.

James 4:8 says, "Draw near to God, and he will draw near to you." Don't let your fears drive you away from His love. He is waiting for you to turn to Him and lean on Him in your time of need.

What fear is breaking your heart?

Pause and tell God how you feel. Move closer to Him and believe that He is drawing near to you.

Psalm 139:7-10, one of today's focal Scriptures, is a journal of David's awareness of God's omnipresence.

Reread Psalm 139:7-10 on page 46. Write the verse you find most meaningful as you think about God's presence in your fears.

Limiting God

Even though God is omnipresent, His Word teaches that He is not with everyone. It is not that God cuts Himself off from certain people but that those people cut themselves off from God. I don't mean you lose your relationship with Him. He is still there, but He withholds His accessible presence. Certain attitudes repel God's intimate presence, just as any sin disrupts your fellowship with Him.

Read the following passages and identify the traits that cut someone off from God's work in their lives.

Psalm 66:18: God is not with those who _____. Why?

Psalm 138:6: God is not with the _____. Why?

Isaiah 1:5,15: God is not with those who _____. Why?

James 4:4: God is not with the _____. Why?

Certain attitudes repel God's intimate presence.

Cherishing iniquity. The idea of cherishing iniquity should disturb us, and yet far too often we repeatedly sin in an area because we find it attractive or enjoyable. In doing so, we are cherishing that wrong action. When we give ourselves to that behavior, we shouldn't expect God to be present.

Harboring pride. Human pride is a thinly veiled claim of divinity. If we insist on ruling even our tiny universe, that sense of distance we will feel indicates separation from God.

Rebelling against God. God will not respond to a rebellious heart. If our hidden intention, even in prayer, is to get God to do what we want rather than His will, our prayers will go unanswered.

Loving the world. God can love the world; we can't. If we give ultimate love to anything other than God, we deprive God of His rightful place of honor in our lives. A friend of the world is an enemy of God.

Are any of your responses to fear creating distance between you and God? Check any of the four attitudes that might be a problem.

- ☐ Iniquity
- ☐ Pride
- ☐ Rebellion
- ☐ Worldliness

God moves any barriers between Him and us to the top of His agenda.

In our interactions with God, He moves any barriers between Him and us to the top of His agenda. Until we get rid of the barrier, everything else becomes secondary. As you face your fears, make sure your heart is right with God by getting rid of any obstacles in your relationship with Him.

Pray through Psalm 139:23-24.

"Search me, O God, and know my heart!
Try me and know my thoughts!
And see if there be any grievous way in me,
and lead me in the way everlasting!"

Repent of anything the Lord shows you that is interfering with your relationship with Him. Ask Him to make you more aware of His intimate presence and strength as you deal with your fears.

Take time to work on this week's memory verse, Deuteronomy 31:6.

Day 4
GOD IS FOR US

Today's Scripture Focus

*"What then shall we say to these things? If God is for us,
who can be against us? He who did not spare his own Son
but gave him up for us all, how will he not also with him graciously
give us all things? Who shall bring any charge against God's elect?
It is God who justifies. Who is to condemn? Christ Jesus is the one
who died—more than that, who was raised—who is at the
right hand of God, who indeed is interceding for us."*

Romans 8:31-34

God is not only with us. He is also for us. And as Romans 8:31 says, "If God is for us, who can be against us?" What problem is too big for Him? What enemy is too strong for Him? Who is going to take you on with God standing beside you? God is for you!

In today's Scripture focus Paul raised several provocative questions and then named specific ways God is for us.

God Gave His Son for Us

Paul first asked, "He who did not spare his own Son but gave him up for us all, how will he not also with him graciously give us all things?" (Rom. 8:32). God gave His only Son for you. His pure, spotless, perfect Son took on Himself the punishment for your sins. There's no better gift than that.

Having an infinite capacity to give and having already given His best, God delights in giving you anything else you ask in His name. Jesus said, "Ask, and it will be given to you; seek, and you will find; knock, and it will be opened to you" (Luke 11:9). Romans 8:34 says Jesus is always at the right hand of God interceding for us. That's why we can come before the throne with boldness and confidence when we ask anything of Him, knowing He will "graciously give us all things" (Rom. 8:32).

One of the greatest implications of God's being for you is that Jesus Himself is praying for you! *This minute.* He talks to the Father about your walk of faith. About your trials. About your fears. Hebrews 7:25 makes this amazing statement: "[Jesus] is able to save to the uttermost those who draw near to God through

God delights in giving you anything else you ask in His name.

him, since he always lives to make intercession for them." Jesus lives to intercede for you. The Greek word for *intercede* conveys the sense of *pleading*; Jesus is continuously and persuasively presenting you and your needs before His Father. Before you ever kneel down to pour out your heart to God, Jesus Christ has already called out to His Father on your behalf. Even before you ask, He knows from firsthand contact what you need—because He is *with* you.

I remember this quotation from my college years: "If you could hear the Lord praying for you in the next room, you would not fear a thousand enemies." Wherever you are this moment, think of the Lord Jesus in the next room, on His knees in front of the couch or a chair. His nail-pierced hands are held out, and He is lifting you and your fears up to His Father. He knows your exact situation. He is asking His Father, "Give her strength." "Give him wisdom." "Give them patience. Remind them they don't have to go it alone. Give them faith that will overcome their fear." Jesus Christ is not only *with* you; He's actually interceding *for* you. And you can be certain that God listens when His Son is praying!

Jesus Christ is not only *with* you; He's actually interceding *for* you.

Describe the burden you feel as you think about your current fears.

What are some things you would want Jesus to pray for you at this time?

How does it make you feel to know that Jesus is talking to the Father about the burdens you are carrying?

As amazing as it is to think that Jesus is praying for us now, the reality is that He started praying for us a long time ago while He was still on earth.

Read John 17:13-21 and list some things Jesus prayed for you.

> "I am coming to you, and these things I speak in the world,
> that they may have my joy fulfilled in themselves. I have given them

your word, and the world has hated them because they are not of the world, just as I am not of the world. I do not ask that you take them out of the world, but that you keep them from the evil one. They are not of the world, just as I am not of the world. Sanctify them in the truth; your word is truth. As you sent me into the world, so I have sent them into the world. And for their sake I consecrate myself, that they also may be sanctified in truth. I do not ask for these only, but also for those who will believe in me through their word, that they may all be one, just as you, Father, are in me, and I in you, that they also may be in us, so that the world may believe that you have sent me."

Things Jesus prayed for me:

All Jesus prayed for His disciples, He also applied to His future followers who would believe because of His disciples' testimonies. That includes you and me!

God Defends Us

Romans 8:33 says, "Who shall bring any charge against God's elect?" Who can accuse us? Who can tear us down before God? God is the One who justifies. He's the Judge. He drops the gavel and makes the final decision. Verse 34 continues, "Who is to condemn? Christ Jesus is the one who died—more than that, who was raised—who is at the right hand of God, who indeed is interceding for us." Jesus knows all about us—every secret insecurity, every private struggle, every vague fear, every stark terror. Romans 8:1 says, "There is therefore now no condemnation for those who are in Christ Jesus." Rather than condemn us, Jesus prays for us. Doesn't that truth cause your spirit to rise up in grateful confidence?

How do your existing fears seek to condemn you?

God Helps Us

Your security is from God.

Earlier this week we read Hebrews 13:5-6: "He has said, 'I will never leave you nor forsake you.' So we can confidently say, 'The Lord is my helper.' " Your security is from God. Your security is not in the stock market, in a successful career, in wise family decisions, in good health, or in your own abilities.

Identify one way fear can result when you place your trust in each of the following.

☐ Financial security:

☐ Career:

☐ Good decisions:

☐ Good health:

☐ Abilities:

All of these things can vanish in a moment. Realizing how tenuous they are can lead directly to fear. But that isn't necessary. God is with you. Even if those other things leave or forsake you, God will be there. You do not have to fear.

Name one fearful situation you are experiencing in which you need to see that God is for you.

How will each of the ways God is for you change your attitude toward your fears?

God gave His Son for you:

God defends you:

God helps you:

You don't need to ask God to be for you. That's a done deal if you're one of His children. Ask Him to open your eyes and your heart to recognize that He is not only everywhere, but He is also everywhere looking out for you!

Practice saying your memory verse for this week, Deuteronomy 31:6.

> **Even if those other things leave or forsake you, God will be there.**

Day 5

TIME FOR STRENGTH AND COURAGE

Today's Scripture Focus

"Be strong and courageous. Do not fear or be in dread of them,
for it is the LORD your God who goes with you.
He will not leave you or forsake you." *Deuteronomy 31:6*

I trust that by now this verse has become embedded in your heart and mind. But we can apply this verse more effectively if we understand its context.

Getting Ready for Battle

Moses and the second generation of the post-Egypt children of Israel were standing on the border of the promised land. Moses knew he was about to die. All of the parents and grandparents of this generation had camped on this very spot almost 40 years before. However, doubt and fear had kept them from entering the promised land. So God had disciplined the nation by making them wander in the wilderness until that generation passed off the scene. Now God was going to give to the children what the parents wouldn't trust Him for. So Moses, on the exit ramp to heaven, delivered these marching orders:

"Before you go up to face those giants in the land, you might think they
are too strong for you, just as your parents thought. But keep in mind
that God is with you. You're going to battle some violent opposition;
you might be tempted to retreat. But reconsider; God is with you.
You'll face overwhelming odds; you'll be incredibly outnumbered.
Fear will be your natural inclination. But keep in mind that God
is with you. This fight is not going to be over in 10 minutes or
10 weeks; there's no quick solution. If you think it's taking too long,
remember that God is with you." *Deuteronomy 31:2-8, my paraphrase*

"Be strong and courageous," the weathered old leader added. "Do not fear or be in dread of them, for it is the LORD your God who goes with you. He will not leave you or forsake you" (Deut. 31:6). I can picture Moses saying, "Haven't we learned this to be true in these 40 years? He never left us while we were in the wilderness. He never forsook us but always provided whatever we needed. Why on earth should you fear now? What He said He would do He has always done!"

What God said He would do He has always done!

The same is true of your battles with fear today. The worse your struggle gets, the more God is with you. The harder the trial, the closer He moves toward you. Are you feeling crushed by fear? God is rushing toward you to stand beside you and go before you into battle.

Where are you in your battle with fear?

☐ Still in Egypt. I haven't even begun to step out in faith.
☐ In the wilderness. God is teaching me what I need to fight my fears.
☐ On the border of the promised land. I'm ready to go into battle because God is with me.

What enemies do you dread or fear as you get ready to move forward?

Facing the Future

In many cases our anticipation of the future is not so much full-blown fear but what we might call low-grade fear that shows up as worry. In the Sermon on the Mount, Jesus addressed fear camouflaged as worry or anxiety that we often allow to undercut our confidence in Him.

Read Matthew 6:25-34 in your Bible. List the sources of anxiety Jesus named.

What did Jesus say to do instead of worrying?

Both Moses and Jesus knew it's not about surviving a particular battle or crisis. It's about seeking God in the face of whatever we are facing. As we learn to trust Him and walk by faith, we are able to fight our fears with His resources. No matter what we face, we don't have to be afraid. We can develop confidence in God's immediate presence in our lives.

> It's not about surviving a particular battle or crisis. It's about seeking God in the face of whatever we are facing.

List the worries or fears that are still uppermost in your mind at present.

Recite this week's memory verse, Deuteronomy 31:6, substituting your fears for the word "them" in the verse.

Commit your remaining fears to God, asking Him to help you move forward in total confidence that He will never leave you or forsake you. Ask Him to increase your faith as you face your fears and trust Him for victory.

Week 3

I WILL NOT DOUBT
GOD IS ALWAYS
IN CONTROL

This Week's Promise

I will not fear; God is always with me.

**I WILL NOT DOUBT;
GOD IS ALWAYS IN CONTROL.**

I will not despair; God is always good.

I will not falter; God is always watching.

I will not fail; God is always victorious.

This Week's Memory Verses

"Trust in the LORD with all your heart,
and do not lean on your own understanding.
In all your ways acknowledge him,
and he will make straight your paths." *Proverbs 3:5-6*

When Questions Come

The Rocky Mountains are about three thousand miles long, extending from the Mexican frontier to the Arctic Circle. Pike's Peak, one of the highest mountains in the Rockies, is almost 14,500 feet tall. When I think of the Rocky Mountains, I think of something ancient, permanent, and immovable. God used mountains as a reference point when He gave us these reassuring words in Isaiah 54:10:

> " 'The mountains may depart
> and the hills be removed,
> but my steadfast love shall not depart from you,
> and my covenant of peace shall not be removed,'
> says the LORD, who has compassion on you."

God was saying that His love for us is everlasting, more solid and stable than the massive Rocky Mountains! We can depend on Him always to be in control.

I have never trusted God and regretted it. But I could fill pages with stories of times when I've doubted God and made bad choices. God has never let me down. His sovereignty has always been at work. You don't have to worry about whether you can trust God. He will be faithful to His character and to His promises.

Christians don't generally set out to doubt God. We don't question our faith without reason. Life's pain or unexpected questions simply catch us off guard. The reality of hardship trips us up. We spiral down fast when we let doubting questions stir our circular reasoning or, even worse, when we listen to other doubters or bitter people. Someone has said that doubt is cancer of the soul. Like a machete to your garden or a wrecking ball against your house, doubt pounds away and damages the structure of the most important thing about you—what you believe about God.

If instead of being caught in the downward spiral of doubt, we take our questions directly to the Lord, our faith increases. Our goal isn't to claim we can't or won't doubt; instead, we need to know what to do with doubts when they come. The promises of God and His character can stand under microscopic scrutiny. Doubts should drive us to God's promises, not cause us to back away from Him. When we say, "I don't know exactly what God is doing, but I know He's in control," that's the unseen evidence of trust in Him.

Week 3

GROUP EXPERIENCE

On the Same Page

1. Identify ads or commercials you have seen that make claims you can't expect to be literally true.

2. What words tip you off that you are being sold something that can't measure up to what is being described?

3. How do exaggerated claims create doubts about other ads or products?

Preparation and Review

1. Last week we talked about not fearing because God is always with us. Share ways you have experienced that truth this week.

2. Most of us have probably had experiences with nagging doubts. What are some stubborn doubts that threaten to disrupt your walk with God?

3. Together read aloud this week's memory verses on page 56.

DVD Session 3 Viewer Guide

Promise 2: I will not _____; God is in _____.

"Trust in the LORD with all your _____" (Prov. 3:5).

Doubt is devastating to your _____.

When I doubt what _____ has said, it's destructive to _____.

When I _____ what God has said, it's really _____ for me.

Consequences of doubt:

1. Doubt is the soil that _____ grows in.
2. Doubt is the cause of our emotional _____ and _____.
3. Doubt is the direct result of taking our eyes off the _____.

58 > ALWAYS TRUE

"Do not lean on your own _____" (Prov. 3:5).

"In all your ways _____ him" (Prov. 3:6).

Conditional promise: if _____ do _____ part, _____ will do _____ part.

"God will make_____ your paths" (Prov. 3:6).

God will _____ the _____ for you.

God promises the safest, fastest, smoothest road to the _____ possible destination.

God is in control means _____.

God's sovereignty:

1. God is sovereign over _____.

2. God is sovereign over _____.

3. God is sovereign over _____ _____.

Responding to the DVD Teaching

1. **Read Proverbs 3:5-6 on page 56. In what ways is God's sovereignty evident in these verses? If He were not sovereign, how would this promise be affected?**

2. **What does it look like to lean on your own understanding? To acknowledge God in all your ways?**

3. **What are you saying about God when you doubt?**

4. **Identify new ways to acknowledge God's sovereignty that you learned from the video segment.**

Read week 3 and complete the activities before the next group experience. Read and recite this week's memory verses, Proverbs 3:5-6, at least once each day this week.

This video session is available for download at *www.lifeway.com/alwaystrue*.

Day 1
I WILL NOT DOUBT

Today's Scripture Focus
"Trust in the Lord with all your heart,
and do not lean on your own understanding.
In all your ways acknowledge him,
and he will make straight your paths."
Proverbs 3:5-6

"Trust in the Lord" in today's Scripture focus is another way to say, "I will not doubt." We can base this conviction on the scriptural promise that God is in control. When we are convinced that God is in control, we can refrain from stepping off the cliff of doubt.

Doubt is a lack of confidence or assurance that God will keep His promises. Doubt always reveals a wrong, distorted, or incomplete view of God. We would do well to practice healthy doubt toward doubts! Our problem is that doubt presents itself as a self-authenticating guide. If we can doubt something, we are tempted to believe it isn't true in spite of the strongest evidence.

God knows when doubts are honest and when they are belligerent rebellion.

God knows when doubts are honest and when they are belligerent rebellion. The desperate father who came to Jesus seeking healing for his son was forced to admit his capacity for uncertainty when they faced each other. The Lord said, " 'All things are possible for one who believes.' Immediately the father of the child cried out and said, 'I believe; help my unbelief!' " Mark (9:23-24).

How would you classify the father's doubt?

☐ A wrong view of God
☐ A distorted view of God
☐ An incomplete view of God

This situation was not a case of a wrong or distorted understanding of God but an incomplete one. The man was simply admitting that although his faith in Jesus was real, it was still shot through with doubts that he desperately wanted help with. God takes special delight in removing doubts that are honestly expressed. This father is a great example of someone who trusted in the Lord rather than leaning on his own understanding.

In contrast, doubt that begins the conversation with assumptions that limit God usually ends up where it started. If we doubt God could have created the world because we are already sure He couldn't have created the world, it's a wasted effort to try to address those doubts. They are already solidified into unbelief.

Identify the three most persistent doubts that nag you in relation to your beliefs about God or your spiritual walk.

1.

2.

3.

How do these doubts affect your day-to-day relationship with God?

How do you usually deal with your doubts? Check all that apply.

- ☐ Try not to think about them
- ☐ Find promises in God's Word to answer them
- ☐ Pray about them
- ☐ Regard them with skepticism
- ☐ Discuss them with another believer
- ☐ Other:

With All Your Heart

When besieged by doubt, we don't have to feel guilty or try to live with it. Proverbs 3:5, part of our Scripture focus today, tells us we can choose to trust God instead of depending on our own understanding of things.

Reread Proverbs 3:5-6 on page 60 and define _trust_ in your own words.

Trust is an active confidence that God's promises are always true. _Trust_ is the verb form of _faith_. We are "faithing" the Lord with all our heart instead of leaning on our own understanding. Trust grows under exposure to the character of God. When we state that we will not doubt because God is in control, we are thinking about God as He has revealed Himself in Jesus Christ, in His Word, and in our lives. Jesus, as God, demonstrated control when it suited the Father's will, including healing diseases, calming storms, and raising the dead. These actions exhibit a lot of control! At the same time, Jesus, as man, demonstrated the willingness to submit even to death under the Father's will, without ever imagining God had lost control of the situation. Acknowledging that God is in control is an essential part of knowing Him.

Acknowledging that God is in control is an essential part of knowing Him.

Reexamine the doubts you listed on page 61. What does each one say about your belief in God's control of the situation?

1.

2.

3.

The phrase in Proverbs 3:5 ".with all your heart" ought to set off recognition bells in our brains. The Great Commandment begins with the phrase "Love the Lord your God with all your heart" (Mark 12:30; also see Deut. 6:5), indicating a close connection between trusting God and loving God. Both are wholehearted responses to God's love and trustworthiness.

Read the following Scriptures and record wrong and right objects of trust.

	Wrong Objects of Trust	Right Objects of Trust
Job 31:24-28		
Psalm 20:7		
Psalm 31:6		
Psalm 40:4		
Psalm 143:8		

What does "with all your heart" look like to you? Identify any activities or commitments you pursue with all your heart.

☐ A sports team   ☐ My relationship with God
☐ My marriage   ☐ My friends
☐ A collection or hobby   ☐ My health
☐ My kids   ☐ My career
☐ A habit
☐ Other:

Only God is worthy of our trust.

Does your passion for a growing relationship with God measure up to your other interests in life? From start to finish, the Bible teaches that our number one focus should be on God. Only He is worthy of our trust. If we go after Him with all our heart, all of our other priorities will line up in their proper order. A focus on God is also the surest way to keep doubts from arising in our spiritual walk.

A Conditional Promise

Proverbs 3:5-6 contains a conditional promise: if we do our part, God will do His part. When we call this promise conditional, we may slip into the error of thinking we're the ones who begin the transaction. We trust, lean not on ourselves, and acknowledge, and then God will make straight our paths. But God does a lot (more like everything) *before* we get a clue about trusting in Him. He makes a lot of moves before we move. He sets up the conditions that make conditional responses possible. Before we ever respond to God in trust, He has already proved Himself trustworthy. We don't trust in the dark or blindly. It's not our trust that causes God to start acting trustworthy. Trustworthy is who God is!

Last week we saw that the generation who witnessed God's amazing action in freeing them from bondage in Egypt refused to trust Him to bring them into the promised land. One of their doubts was that God would allow their children to suffer the same fate in Canaan they had suffered in Egypt, and they would end up as slaves in a new place. They asked Moses and Aaron, "Why is the Lord bringing us into this land, to fall by the sword? Our wives and our little ones will become a prey. Would it not be better for us to go back to Egypt?" (Num. 14:3). This response drew God's ire, and He threatened to destroy them. But after Moses intervened for the people, God let them know He wasn't going to stop being trustworthy because of their doubts. Although they would die in the wilderness for their unbelief, their children would one day receive the promised land: "Your little ones, who you said would become a prey, I will bring in, and they shall know the land that you have rejected" (14:31).

A conditional promise usually means active participation on our part. But our action isn't blind faith. We can act because God is trustworthy. If we reject doubt and choose to trust God, we will see His promises come to pass.

> **If we reject doubt and choose to trust God, we will see His promises come to pass.**

How has God proved Himself trustworthy in your life? Think of past trials as well as His guidance of your life path.

What have you learned about God that would help you refute any doubts you are having now?

Getting Out of the Boat

James wrote, "The one who doubts is like a wave of the sea that is driven and tossed by the wind" (Jas. 1:6). Those who doubt are unstable in their Christian lives. Like a wave, they rock back and forth in a constant state of disruption.

Peter is the patron saint of all of us who waver back and forth in our faith walk. For most of us, the journey toward trust is never just forward. We all have moments of panic, retreat, and failure—just like Peter.

Read the account in Matthew 14:22-33 of Jesus and Peter's walk among the waves.

Who had more trust, Peter or the disciples who stayed on the boat? Why?

At what point did Peter run into trouble?

What has happened in your life when you have taken your eyes off the Lord?

As you think about any doubts you are dealing with, in what ways do you need to step out of the boat and ask God to let you walk on water? Are you facing a financial flood tide? Does your marriage seem headed for the rocks? Are you lost at sea when it comes to raising your children? What could you do to step out in complete trust in God?

Will I trust my doubts, or will I trust the Lord?

Peter is a great example of a faith walk because he kept moving forward even when he fell flat on his face. He continued trusting even when he had a lot more to learn about trusting. When we trust God enough to get out of the boat, we have to keep trusting Him to walk on the water. Like Peter, we are constantly confronted with a choice: will I trust my doubts, or will I trust the Lord?

As you continue this week's study, ask God to help you put off doubt and trust Him with all your heart. Ask Him to allow you to step boldly outside the boat and onto the waves, totally depending on Him to carry you through.

Begin memorizing this week's memory verses, Proverbs 3:5-6.

Day 2

GOD IS SOVEREIGN

Today's Scripture Focus

"In all your ways acknowledge him,
and he will make straight your paths."

Proverbs 3:6

God is in control. In theological terms it means He is sovereign, which means He is in charge of all He created; He rules as supreme Lawgiver and Sustainer. Faced with our obvious lack of control, we find God's sovereignty a continual mystery. In our fallenness we sometimes resort to two serious mistakes.

1. We give God credit for His control over certain areas while we quietly seek to maintain control over personal areas. "Lord, You go ahead and run the universe. I'll take care of my little thing over here." We declare a partnership with God, but we're really in charge of everything that concerns us.

2. We grudgingly admit God is in control and then try to get leverage to control Him. It's all right if God is in charge as long as He's doing what we want Him to do. "Lord, You are running everything, but You seem to be slipping up in my life. You're in control of the vehicle, but it isn't going where I want to go." Those mixed-message prayers may sound as if we're acknowledging God, but we are addressing Him only for the purpose of control.

In All Your Ways

Today's Scripture focus says we must acknowledge God in *all* our ways. How do we do that? Acknowledgment doesn't just mean admitting God is there. There are plenty of people who vaguely acknowledge there's probably someone or a power out there who is greater than we—but they want nothing to do with Him! That's not the kind of acknowledgment that invites God to make our paths straight.

In every person's life there are a fair number of bumps in the road. There's stuff we have to climb over and a ton of concerns that weigh us down. We each have our own list. There are times when all we can see are the hard road and the heavy load. But the Lord promises if we trust in Him with all our heart, if we do not lean on our own understanding, and if we acknowledge Him in all our ways, He will make our paths smooth. God will pave the way for us.

God is in charge of all He created.

Describe what it means to acknowledge God in all your ways.

The kind of acknowledgment that unleashes the road-grading, asphalt-spreading, pathway-straightening heavy equipment is a learned humility that says, "Lord, You are God, and I am definitely not!" We have to admit God is in control and deliberately take our hands off the controls. We don't just acknowledge He's there. We step aside and deliberately say, "Lord, not my will but Yours be done."

When was the last time you intentionally acknowledged God in the middle of a decision or an action? What happened as a result of that acknowledgment?

Have you deliberately acknowledged God's control over the doubts in your life? ☐ Yes ☐ No

You can measure the degree to which you have placed your doubts in God's hands by recognizing what you do when they come to mind. When the problem comes to mind, do you instantly switch into the grateful "I'm glad this is in Your hands, Lord" mode, or do you start working on it, taking charge of it again?

Perfect Peace

The problem with trying to be in control of life is that you don't have a moment's rest. You've got to be *on* 24/7. Things can spin out of control at a moment's notice (and they often do), so you have to carry this heavy responsibility of running everything. Most of us know we can't handle this load, but we think if we can just control enough, we'll have some peace.

Read Isaiah 26:3.

> "You keep him in perfect peace
> whose mind is stayed on you,
> because he trusts in you."

According to this verse, what is the source of peace?

How does this verse say peace is achieved?

Do you think this peace can coexist with doubt? Why or why not?

> You can measure the degree to which you have placed your doubts in God's hands by recognizing what you do when they come to mind.

In this verse "whose mind is stayed on you" is another way of saying, "In all your ways acknowledge Him." In the midst of life's turmoil, God promises perfect peace if we keep our minds on Him. His divine peace will never happen if we insist on maintaining control.

Life can sometimes get chaotic. To assert that God is in control when life feels like a tornado on steroids may seem like the last thing you want to say, but it often creates an instant calm in the storm. But God's control doesn't mean there are no terrible storms in life any more than God's control of the created order means there shouldn't be wind and rain storms. We batten down the hatches while we acknowledge God is in control.

Maybe you know some things. You've been around the block. You know how processes work. You know how to get certain tasks done. There's nothing wrong with that. The problem is when you lean on those things when you hit a crisis or face doubts. Are you placing your confidence in your own ability to get out of tight spots? Don't lean on your own understanding. If your trust in God is limited by your own understanding, you will always have limited trust.

> **If your trust in God is limited by your own understanding, you will always have limited trust.**

What are some areas of life in which you tend to rely on your own expertise rather than on God?

What are some areas of life in which you know you need to rely on God?

How do your current doubts make you recognize your dependence on God?

Mature believers recognize that even when it appears we have everything under control, we could quickly go under if we relied on our own abilities or went our own way. Even when our abilities seem to be working, we must acknowledge that God is the source of those abilities! Keeping our minds stayed on God is the only way to maintain a walk of trust. When we acknowledge God's control, He guarantees the safest, fastest, smoothest road to the best possible destination: peace for the journey and ultimate peace when we arrive at our destination.

End today's study by praying about your doubts. Instead of leaning on your own understanding, acknowledge God's control in these situations. Lean on His strong, supporting arms.

Practice saying this week's memory verses, Proverbs 3:5-6.

SOVEREIGN OVER THE UNIVERSE

Today's Scripture Focus

"He is the image of the invisible God, the firstborn of all creation. For by him all things were created, in heaven and on earth, visible and invisible, whether thrones or dominions or rulers or authorities— all things were created through him and for him. And he is before all things, and in him all things hold together."

Colossians 1:15-17

I recently got a great e-mail from my dad. At the end he wrote, "Will be in unceasing prayer for you and yours on every front known to me and of course through other fronts I know little or nothing of but God my Father knows in full detail and has under His sovereign control." My dad is a great believer. He knows all about the sovereignty of God.

We have a God who is in complete control.

If you want to comfort your heart when you have doubts and have something to give to another believer who is doubting, you've got to understand the biblical doctrine of the sovereignty of God. No matter what happens or comes our way, we have a God who is in complete control. And there's no better place to start than with His control over His grand project we call creation.

Sovereign over Creation

When the apostle Paul preached the gospel to the philosophers in Athens, he established common ground for a spiritual conversation with them by stating basic assumptions about God's control that he felt his audience would agree with. The account in Acts 17 is fascinating, particularly Paul's comment in verses 24-25: "The God who made the world and everything in it, being Lord of heaven and earth, does not live in temples made by man, nor is he served by human hands, as though he needed anything, since he himself gives to all mankind life and breath and everything."

God doesn't live in our church buildings. He doesn't hang out there all week while we go about our lives. He inhabits the entire universe. He is familiar with every nook, cranny, black hole, and galaxy. He created it all and manages every part of it. Throughout the Old Testament we see God commanding and ruling

His creation. With His mighty hand He brought plagues on Egypt and parted the waters of the Red Sea so that His people could cross over as a free people.

Our Scripture focus today tells us that as God's Son, Jesus was the agent of creation: "By him all things were created, in heaven and on earth, visible and invisible, whether thrones or dominions or rulers or authorities—all things were created through him and for him. And he is before all things, and in him all things hold together" (Col. 1:16-17). When Jesus was on earth, He demonstrated power over His creation the same way His Father did in the Old Testament. Read what happens in this story from the life of Christ.

> "When he got into the boat, his disciples followed him.
> And behold, there arose a great storm on the sea, so that the boat
> was being swamped by the waves; but he was asleep. And they went
> and woke him, saying, 'Save us, Lord; we are perishing.' And he said
> to them, 'Why are you afraid, O you of little faith?' Then he rose
> and rebuked the winds and the sea, and there was a great calm.
> And the men marveled, saying, 'What sort of man is this,
> that even winds and sea obey him?' " *Matthew 8:23-27*

What did Jesus identify as the problem with the way the disciples looked at their predicament?

These men had walked with Jesus for a while. Why do you think they were surprised by this demonstration of His power?

Have you ever responded as the disciples did in verse 27 when Jesus came through for you?

The disciples' after-action report is revealing: "What sort of man is this, that even winds and sea obey him?" (v. 27). Those disciples had already seen Jesus do a lot, like healing physical diseases and expelling demons. Now Jesus had raised the bar considerably. The disciples exclaimed their amazement over the revelation that the One they already believed in as God's Messiah was doing exactly what God would do in taking control of nature.

There are no illusions here. This is God we're talking about. He has said, "Is anything too hard for the LORD?" (Gen. 18:14). He can handle anything that's

When Jesus was on earth, He demonstrated power over His creation the same way His Father did in the Old Testament.

in your path. When you invited Jesus into your heart, you gained access to that divine power. Because "in him all things hold together" (Col. 1:17), Jesus is deeply involved in your life. He controls the universe. Is there ever any reason to doubt His ability to see you through your trials and doubts?

Think about the doubts you are currently dealing with. Check any of the following questions you can ask yourself as reminders that God is in control.

☐ What is it about this situation that Jesus can't control?
☐ Is anything too hard for the Lord?
☐ Am I going to have to help God work this out?
☐ Who could help me more than God in this situation?
☐ When did God lose control of things?
☐ Other:

How do the questions you checked specifically target your tendency to doubt?

Sovereign over Humanity

A teenage girl having a little fun once dove into a lake without checking for unseen objects in the water. She struck her head, and immediately her carefree body was transformed into an almost immovable set of arms and legs. Facing a lifetime as a quadriplegic, she was gripped by the inevitable questions: Where was God when she was heading into the water? When the possibility of normal is removed, how much can God still do? Joni Eareckson Tada would say it's amazing what God can do. By trusting Him in her doubts and suffering, she has been able to influence and encourage thousands of people through her decades-long ministry and testimony.

We assume an unexpected turn in the road that we label hard means another way would have been easier, when it might have proved harder, darker, and wrong. The way not taken is never the best way when we acknowledge that God is in control—not only over creation but also over our individual lives.

Paul continued his address to the Athenians, "He [God] made from one man [Adam] every nation of mankind to live on all the face of the earth, having

> The way not taken is never the best way when we acknowledge that God is in control.

determined allotted periods and the boundaries of their dwelling place. For, 'In him we live and move and have our being' " (Acts 17:26,28). God is Lord of nations, of races, of governments. And He has a purpose for the way He has determined us to live on this earth: "They should seek God, in the hope that they might feel their way toward him and find him" (v. 27).

Think back on your life and write a couple of ways God brought you to a relationship with Himself.

How can you see God working in your life at present in spite of the doubts you are struggling with?

If we focus on our doubts without keeping our minds set on God, we make it harder for God to work in our lives. But if we place the full weight of our trust in Him, He will be faithful to grow our faith in spite of our doubts.

Ephesians 1:11 says God "works all things according to the counsel of his will." God rules the universe, and He orders the events of our lives. He is God no matter what we might think or what our opinions might be about Him. He is larger than our limited definitions of Him. God is so in control that He rules the universe with His feet up. He's not stressed or strained in any way. He's not pacing back and forth. He doesn't wipe sweat from His brow. There is no world problem that stretches Him. He is God, and He is sovereign.

> If we place the full weight of our trust in God, He will be faithful to grow our faith in spite of our doubts.

Spend time praising God for His sovereignty. Submit your doubts to Him and confess that He is in control of your circumstances and your life.

Practice reciting your memory verses for this week, Proverbs 3:5-6.

SOVEREIGN OVER THE MORAL UNIVERSE

Today's Scripture Focus

"Joseph said to them, 'Do not fear, for am I in the place of God?
As for you, you meant evil against me, but God meant it for good,
to bring it about that many people should be kept alive,
as they are today. So do not fear; I will provide for you and your
little ones.' Thus he comforted them and spoke kindly to them."

Genesis 50:19-21

People get away with murder—literally as well as figuratively! Or so it seems until we push back the curtain and remember that not everything will be settled in this life. God will have the last word on the matter of justice. Our common insistence on vengeance and fairness in this life is often a thinly veiled belief that God can't be trusted in responding to sinful behavior. We are tempted to take things into our hands or keep offenses alive in our hearts. Not only that, but what may look to us like someone blissfully escaping the consequences of bad behavior may in fact be someone racked by guilt or undergoing unseen chastening from God.

God will have the last word on the matter of justice.

Describe a time when you wanted or insisted on immediate justice in this life. What doubts about God lay behind this desire?

Sovereign over Sin

If you ever need a hero in the "I will not doubt: God is always in control" club, Joseph would have to be a serious candidate (see Gen. 37–50). After being threatened with death and sold to slave traders by his brothers, Joseph ended up in Egypt honoring God with his life, trusting the Lord, making decisions of faith, and not leaning on his own understanding. But even then he was unfairly harassed, falsely accused, and thrown into prison. It seemed as if his days were over, but again, God was in control.

Years later, still in prison, Joseph was working hard, still trusting the Lord, still believing God's ways were best, and not leaning on human wisdom—and it seemed he was finally going to catch a break. But this time it was his new friends who betrayed him. The restored cupbearer forgot he was stuck in the dungeon, and again his future looked grim. But then God stepped in and demonstrated in amazing detail that He was sovereign over the sins of Joseph's brothers, the false accusers, and the betraying friends.

In the end Joseph was elevated to a position of authority in the Egyptian government. Even Pharaoh recognized God's hand on Joseph's life and said to his servants, "Can we find a man like this, in whom is the Spirit of God?" (Gen. 41:38). In God's timing Joseph's brothers eventually stood before him, bowing in honor with their hands out, asking for bread. Nobody but God could have orchestrated a story with so many twists. You can imagine how terrified Joseph's brothers were when they realized they now bowed before their little brother whom they had abused years earlier. But Joseph knew about the sovereignty of God. He looked his brothers in the eyes and said, "You meant evil against me, but God meant it for good" (50:20). That is an awesome truth: God can use even the sin of other people to accomplish His purposes in your life.

> **God can use even the sin of other people to accomplish His purposes in your life.**

We wonder how many times Joseph persistently confessed his trust in God's sovereignty as time after time his life seemed to take detours in the wrong direction. Repeated, devastating, personal disasters occurred that might have caused him to think, *Hey, Lord, what are You doing? I'm having a hard time seeing that You're in control right now.* Yet Joseph kept landing on his feet and trusting God in every turn of events. This case study of triumph over tragedy is a sobering testament to God's control over the moral universe.

Describe a time in your life when someone mistreated you, but God worked things out for your good anyway.

Are any of your present doubts caused by a wrong someone has committed against you? ☐ **Yes** ☐ **No**

Are you able to turn this situation over to God, trusting His sovereign ability to bring about justice according to His time and purposes? ☐ **Yes** ☐ **No**

Sovereign in Waiting

Notice Joseph had to wait a very long time to see good come from his suffering. The same may be true in our lives. The only problem with waiting is ... well, the waiting part. If we were convinced we were going to get instant gratification, we would be more willing to trust God's promises. We may not put it into words, but our track record often tells God, "All right, Lord, I'm trusting You! The clock is ticking; You now have two minutes to come through for me big-time! If I don't get an overnight FedEx delivery from You, I'm exercising my relapse-to-doubt option!" We love the happy ending of Joseph's story, but it's the delayed fulfillment that drives us crazy. God gave Joseph a couple of specific dreams as a young man that seemed to be mocked at every turn. Most of us at least have an open-ended promise that God will make a way for us. Joseph, on the other hand, had to deal with the repeated disappointment that nothing in his surroundings vaguely indicated he was anywhere near seeing those dreams fulfilled.

How long have you been struggling with your three biggest doubts you identified on page 61?

1. _____ 2. _____ 3. _____

Doubt tends to grow when we have to wait. Things that were seemingly insignificant questions one day become entrenched concerns the next. Think about all the evidence of God's presence the Israelites had seen by the time they reached Mount Sinai. God had powerfully intervened in their suffering to deliver them from Pharaoh's hand. He had miraculously parted the Red Sea for their escape, provided manna and quail for their sustenance, and led them in a cloud by day and in fire by night. But now Moses had been on Mount Sinai for weeks, and doubt began to take root in the people's minds. "Up, make us gods who shall go before us," they concluded. "As for this Moses, the man who brought us up out of the land of Egypt, we do not know what has become of him" (Ex. 32:1). The Israelites' walk of faith was soon exchanged for wholesale idol worship and immorality. Unchecked doubt will take us where we don't want to go!

God's promises allow us to walk by faith while we are waiting for Him to work. And He will in His time. But we've got to take His promises as His bond. He has told us what He will do, and He has promised, "We know that for those who love God all things work together for good, for those who are called according to his purpose" (Rom. 8:28). Our job is to trust that He is in control, allowing Him to increase our faith and to bring about all the good He desires for us.

God's promises allow us to walk by faith while we are waiting for Him to work.

Sovereign over Rebellion

Standing in stark contrast to Joseph is Jonah, the patron saint of the "Lord, I've got a better idea" crowd. Most of us join that club almost as soon as we become Christians: "Lord, thank You so much for saving me! I will be eternally grateful that You rescued me from sin and gave me a new life now and forever. Now I'll take it from here if You don't mind." Unfortunately, this attitude is the opposite of acknowledging God in all our ways (see Prov. 3:6).

It all started when God instructed Jonah to go to Nineveh to deliver His message of repentance. Jonah decided he wasn't going. How was rebellion going to work out for Jonah? Not great. Jonah booked a cruise going west instead of east, so all of a sudden out of nowhere "the LORD hurled a great wind upon the sea" (Jonah 1:4). When Jonah admitted he was the reason for the storm, the crew, afraid for their lives, threw him overboard. But was God done with Jonah yet? No.

Jonah 1:17 tells us, "The LORD appointed a great fish to swallow up Jonah." Jonah prayed to the Lord in the belly of the fish, and he was spit out on dry land. Immediately Jonah set out for Nineveh. In the end, despite His prophet's lackluster performance, God brought a sweeping revival to those wicked people. Even after all he had been through, Jonah chose to be discouraged and depressed because he didn't think Ninevites deserved God's mercy. It was apparently going to take more than three days in a fish to knock Jonah's pride and rebellion out of his heart. Jonah was so angry, in fact, that he said, "O LORD, please take my life from me, for it is better for me to die than to live" (4:3). Now that's pouting with an attitude! And God, in His tender love, responded by asking him, "Do you do well to be angry?"(4:4). The Lord "appointed a plant and made it come up over Jonah, that it might be a shade over his head, to save him from his discomfort" (4:6). But God also sent a worm to gnaw on the plant, and it died. Jonah was mad! Again the Lord came to him and asked, "Do you do well to be angry?" (4:9). Jonah said, "I do well to be angry, angry enough to die" (4:9). Seriously, Jonah had some major problems. Yet the Lord was so tender and loving toward Him that He went to work on his heart just as certainly as He had pursued the people of Nineveh. God is sovereign even over rebellion.

It was apparently going to take more than three days in a fish to knock Jonah's pride and rebellion out of his heart.

Holding out for our will against God's will is a major challenge for us. Rebellion is sin. And because God retains control over His moral universe, we can be sure our rebellion will bring about painful consequences, shame, and regrets. But it will not alter God's will an inch to the right or left.

Identify a time when you rebelled instead of obeying what God wanted you to do.

How did God bring you to repentance and bring about His will in spite of your rebellion?

Think about the doubts you have identified this week. Which of them spring from an attitude of rebellion in your life?

Write this week's memory verses, Proverbs 3:5-6.

How would rebellion affect your ability to obey each phrase in those verses?

Everything God does has our ultimate benefit in mind.

It's easy to assume that we're in an unfair wrestling match with God, and He always wins. He gets His way sooner or later. The fact that we resent this arrangement can remind us that we're still short of understanding the essential goodness of God exercised on our behalf. Often we can only imagine Him saying, "Don't!" all the time without realizing that He always means, "Don't hurt yourself!" Everything God does has our ultimate benefit in mind.

Make your closing prayer today one of surrender. Ask God to point out rebellious streaks in you. Raise a white flag over your life that carries this inscription in red: "Not my will, Lord, but Yours be done—always."

Day 5

SOVEREIGN OVER HISTORY

Today's Scripture Focus

"When God desired to show more convincingly to the heirs
of the promise the unchangeable character of his purpose,
he guaranteed it with an oath, so that by two unchangeable things,
in which it is impossible for God to lie, we who have fled for refuge
might have strong encouragement to hold fast to the hope set
before us. We have this as a sure and steadfast anchor of the soul."

Hebrews 6:17-19

Do you find that newspaper headlines and teaser ads for the television news provoke you to doubt? "The world is coming apart at the seams! Total chaos seems eminent! Things couldn't be worse! Film at 11:00!" You can be sure God never gets upset over the news and changes the channel. So if we have His perspective, no matter what the news is, the scroll that should be running at the bottom of our mental screens is "I will not doubt; God is always in control."

Christians have the advantage of viewing world events through a God filter. Wars and disasters have punctuated history, but rather than assume those events are evidence of a world out of control, we should ask questions like: What were believers doing while this was going on? How did God stand with those who trusted in Him? What did believers discover about God when they chose not to doubt but trusted that God was always in control?

> **Christians have the advantage of viewing world events through a God filter.**

What are the top three current world events or situations that tend to discourage you most?

1.

2.

3.

What are some biblical truths that give you hope when the world seems to be spinning out of control?

God is orchestrating
the events of history
to bring about a
meaningful and
victorious conclusion
for His people.

The world is spiraling down, writhing in the death throes of sin. But the future belongs to God's people. Scripture assures us that God is orchestrating the events of history to bring about a meaningful and victorious conclusion for His people. Jesus will return to bring judgment, to destroy sin and death, and to establish an eternal kingdom of peace and righteousness. In the meantime the news reports might appall us, making us wonder, *How much worse can things get?* But they don't need to make us doubt that God is in control. He has much better things planned for us, and we can trust Him for that.

A Showdown Between Good and Evil

Elijah, one of the greatest prophets in the Old Testament, wasn't immune to doubt and discouragement when facing the forces of evil. Even though God was doing great things through him, he was still personally affected by appearances rather than reality. At the time, God was using a drought in the promised land to get the attention of His people, who had turned away from Him. Elijah had announced this forecast, and God was demonstrating His control over the natural order by withholding rain (see 1 Kings 17:1-7).

So one week Elijah participated in a historic showdown with 450 prophets of Baal, a pagan god who was all the rage in Israel at the time. The showdown with the Baal team, who were backed up by Queen Jezebel's personal gang of Asherah prophets, turned into a humiliating and deadly rout for the bad guys. Scratch 850 pagan prophets. The fire God sent from heaven to ignite the water-soaked wood, sacrifice, and altar sort of got everyone's attention. Then, to clean up the mess, God opened the reservoirs of heaven and sent rain to the nation. These were pretty conclusive indications that God was fully capable not only of managing the created order but also of working in human events.

But as Elijah was basking in success, he made the mistake of reading the *Jerusalem Post* headlines: "Queen Vows Elijah Is Toast!" Instead of laughing and saying, "Bring it!" Elijah panicked and ran. After all of the amazing things he had witnessed God do, he blinked when it got personal and let doubt overtake him. Maybe he was emotionally tired from all the excitement. Or perhaps he was disappointed that just when everything seemed to be leading to a happily-ever-after conclusion, danger reared its ugly head. So Elijah ran off to the desert. Ready to give up, he lay down under a broom tree to die, but God had other plans. He turned that corner of the wilderness into a 40-day spa retreat for Elijah, taking care of all of his needs.

When Elijah had physically recovered, God confronted his spiritual attitude. It turns out that Elijah was suffering from an advanced case of "I'm the last man standing" syndrome. God had to teach Elijah two lessons: (1) even if Elijah was the only one left, with God that would have been more than enough; (2) not counting Elijah, God had "seven thousand in Israel, all the knees that have not bowed to Baal, and every mouth that has not kissed him" (1 Kings 19:18). These go-to people were further proof that God was fully in control of world events.

In your most recent bout with doubt, worry, or self-pity, to what degree can you now see the cause was your attempt to take control of things that God was in charge of?

When are you most in danger of succumbing to doubt—after a great success or in the middle of a hard time? Why?

No matter when doubts attack us, God's promises provide us with a safe refuge. Today's Scripture focus, Hebrews 6:17-19, definitely applies to all of God's promises: "When God desired to show more convincingly to the heirs of the promise the unchangeable character of his purpose, he guaranteed it with an oath, so that by two unchangeable things, in which it is impossible for God to lie, we who have fled for refuge might have strong encouragement to hold fast to the hope set before us. We have this as a sure and steadfast anchor of the soul." In this passage the writer of Hebrews was talking about God's promise to Abraham of a nation and a blessing. Responding to God in faith, Abraham patiently waited for and obtained the promise.

> No matter when doubts attack us, God's promises provide us with a safe refuge.

Like Abraham, you have great and precious promises from God that provide a dependable attachment point for your soul. When the waves are crazy high and the wind whips strong and cold across your face and you don't know what's going to happen, you have an anchor in the storm. You have the assurance that God is in control and has made promises He has guaranteed with an oath. You don't know when those promises will happen, but you can be sure they will. That kind of assurance will settle your heart right down.

What do you think the "two unchangeable things" are in Hebrews 6:18?

- ☐ Abraham and God
- ☐ God's desire and God's oath
- ☐ God's oath and God's promise
- ☐ God's purpose and God's character

Since God cannot lie, what does that fact say about His promises?

How are God's promises becoming for you "a sure and steadfast anchor of the soul" when you face doubts and hard times?

Because God cannot lie, His promises are set in stone.

You were correct if you checked the second, third, or fourth choice in the last activity on page 79. The unchangeable part of the equation resided in God, not in Abraham. Because God cannot lie, His promises are set in stone. You can always trust them to be an anchor for your soul.

God's Unchanging Purpose

If Jezebel was at one end of the continuum of queens, Esther occupies the opposite end of that continuum. Jezebel lived in blatant disregard for God's Word and God's people; Esther was a woman after God's own heart. The story of Esther contains numerous examples of ways God controls events even when we don't notice His working behind the scenes.

In telling this historical account, under divine inspiration, the author chose not to mention God's name in recording the events that swirled around Esther. But don't miss God's fingerprints all over the events, lining up people and circumstances in perfect timing to preserve His people and establish His control.

This episode of epic proportions shows God winning over evil. Satan's tool was a man named Haman, who, not surprisingly, hated God's people. He wielded his power and influence with the king to legalize a plan that would annihilate the Jews. The Jews were helpless against the law, except that in God's plan two Jewish persons stood in Haman's way. The first was Mordecai, who faithfully held his ground, completely enraging Haman.

The other was Mordecai's cousin, Esther. Odd circumstances and the whims of others had surprisingly landed her in the king's palace. Chosen to be in the king's harem, she was eventually named the queen. But she kept secret the fact that she was a Jew. When the heinous plot to exterminate the Jews became law, Mordecai saw God's plan right away. It was no accident that Esther lived in the palace and could influence the king. But when Esther hesitated, fearing repercussions if the king didn't receive her well, Mordecai gave her a great lesson in God's sovereignty: "Do not think to yourself that in the king's palace you will escape any more than all the other Jews. For if you keep silent at this time, relief and deliverance will rise for the Jews from another place, but you and your father's house will perish"

(Esth. 4:13-14). God will have His way. If you don't do it, He will find someone who will. No matter what, God's purpose will be accomplished.

Mordecai continued, "Who knows whether you have not come to the kingdom for such a time as this?" (v. 14). All of the events of Esther's life brought her to this place in history. God knew what He was doing in the life of the nation of Israel. His purpose would not be thwarted. Esther took a stand for God's people, and God used her courage and obedience to preserve them.

Looking back on your life, how can you see God's sovereign hand directing the circumstances, relationships, and events of your past?

How has God used doubts and hard times you have experienced to show you His purposes and to teach you more about Himself?

God is sovereign not only over history and world events but also over each individual. Nothing others have done could thwart God's plan for your life. No circumstance can change what God purposes to do. In fact, the events that have frustrated, hurt, and derailed your plans may be some of the clearest clues about God's plans for you—sometimes even more obvious than His blessings.

> Nothing others have done could thwart God's plan for your life.

Christians have the freedom of seeing the biggest picture of all. We are not even limited by time. Neither is God. Things we hope for may not work out while we are on earth, but we have to trust God for their ultimate resolution. Because of Jesus' death and resurrection, we now see our own death as a doorway rather than the end of the line. Those who die with the most toys have won nothing. Those who seem to get away with something in this life have gotten away with nothing. Everything will be settled in God's time. He is always in control. You can trust Him to work out everything for your good.

Pray about any doubts that still bother you and express your trust in God to work out His purposes for your good.

Quote your memory verses for this week, Proverbs 3:5-6.

Week 4

I WILL NOT DESPAIR
GOD IS ALWAYS
GOOD

This Week's Promise

I will not fear; God is always with me.

I will not doubt; God is always in control.

I WILL NOT DESPAIR; GOD IS ALWAYS GOOD.

I will not falter; God is always watching.

I will not fail; God is always victorious.

This Week's Memory Verse

"We know that for those who love God all things work together for good, for those who are called according to his purpose." *Romans 8:28*

A Walk on the Beach

The ocean covers 71 percent of the earth's surface. Its average depth is about 12,000 feet, and the deepest part, the Mariana Trench, plummets seven miles into the Pacific Ocean. Habakkuk 2:14 prophesies,

> "The earth will be filled
> with the knowledge of the glory of the LORD
> as the waters cover the sea."

Standing on the shore at sunrise or sunset, you sense the glory of the Lord who created the ocean and all of the creatures that live in it. Since the moment God formed it and divinely set it in motion, the ocean has never ceased its endless journey as its waves relentlessly break on shore hour after hour, day after day, according to the faithful pattern of the tides. God's goodness is like that—relentless and faithful. Like the breaking of the waves, His goodness keeps coming at us no matter what trial or problem threatens to overwhelm us with despair. His unfailing Word guarantees it.

The first two issues we looked at in this study involved what, for many of us, are momentary experiences: fear and doubt. These regularly come and go in our lives. When they come knocking at our door, God's promises give us the backbone to keep the door closed. The next three issues we will examine tend to be more persistent problems than fear or doubt. Despair, faltering, and failure are more than minor distractions that stop by to visit once in a while. These are enemies that lay siege to our well-being. They make us feel as if we are surrounded with no way of escape. We may not even know we've been endangered until our defenses are breached. And if we let any of these three have a greater say in our thinking and actions than we allow Christ and His Word, we are in for a long, dark time.

The powerful weapon we have to repel this invader called despair is the powerful promise that God is always good. When our struggles seem overwhelming, we can take a mental walk on the beach and let the promise of God's goodness wash over our being. To believe that promise is to see the glory of the Lord.

Week 4

GROUP EXPERIENCE

despair is not reality

despair : destitute of positive expectation

On the Same Page

1. What is one of your favorite stories of a sports team that made a great comeback, snatching victory out of the jaws of defeat? If you were on the eventual winning team, describe the range of emotions you went through between the time when the score looked insurmountable and when victory was achieved.

2. Now think of a time when a sports team appeared to be on the verge of victory, only to experience a stunning reversal and loss. Describe the reactions of the players and fans. How did the element of surprise increase the team's despair?

Preparation and Review

1. We have now memorized three promise verses: 2 Peter 1:3-4; Deuteronomy 31:6; and Proverbs 3:5-6. Test your memories by reciting these verses together.

2. Together read aloud this week's memory verse on page 82.

3. What pictures come to mind when you hear the word *despair*? What are some causes of despair in our world today?

DVD Session 4 Viewer Guide

Promise 3: I will not __despair__ ; God is _____.

I will not __despair__.

Despair: destitute of positive __expectation__

Despair is not __reality__, but to the person who is there, they __believe__ it is reality.

Accelerants for despair:

1. __surprise__
2. __severity__
3. __settledness__

"I would have despaired unless I had _____believed_____" (Ps. 27:13).

When you can't do anything at all, you let __God__ do it.

"Stand firm, and see the salvation of the LORD. ... The LORD will __fight__ for you, and you have only to be _____silent_____" (Ex. 14:13-14).

Isaih 30:15

Psalm 46:10

"I would have despaired unless I had believed that I would _see_" (Ps. 27:13).
"... the goodness of the LORD in the land of the _____living_____" (Ps. 27:13).

In your lifetime you will see the _____goodness_____ of the Lord.

God is always __good__.

God's goodness:

1. God's goodness is something He wants us to _experience_ (see Ps. 34:8).
2. God's goodness is the eventual conclusion of every generation
   of His _____followers_____ (see Ps. 100:5).
3. God's goodness is present in _____everything_____ He does (see Ps. 145:9).
4. God's goodness is not immediately _____apparent_____ (see Lam. 3:25).
5. God's goodness is a _____refuge_____, and He is aware of those who find
   Him (see Nah. 1:7).

God has a __plan__ for your life.

"I __know__ the plans I have for you" (Jer. 29:11).
Plans for _____wholeness_____ and not for _evil_ (see Jer. 29:11)
"... to give you a _____future_____ and a __hope__" (Jer. 29:11).

God is working all things together (see Rom. 8:28):

(1) For my __good__ and (2) for His _____purpose_____

Responding to the DVD Teaching

1. What would you like to say about the goodness of the Lord right now?

**2. Review the facts we know about God's plans for us in Jeremiah 29:11.
Which one means the most to you today and why?**

**Read week 4 and complete the activities before the next group experience. Read
and recite this week's memory verse, Romans 8:28, at least once each day this week.**

This video session is available for download at *www.lifeway.com/alwaystrue.*

I WILL NOT DESPAIR

Today's Scripture Focus

"I would have despaired unless I had believed
that I would see the goodness of the Lord
In the land of the living."
Psalm 27:13, NASB

When I was a kid, our family spent summer holidays traveling all over Canada and the United States, pulling our little camper-trailer behind our car. One place I vividly remember visiting was Carlsbad Caverns. I recall hiking down, down, down into the deepest tunnels, more than 1,600 feet into the earth. The deeper we went, the darker and damper it got. Though the New Mexico desert floor sweltered above us, we got so cold and clammy down there that we were thankful for sweaters. My brothers and I spooked out one another by imagining how scary it would be if the electricity went out and the artificial light and air circulation shut off while we were deep in the caverns. That picture comes to mind when I think of despair. It's that crushing awareness that you are deep down in a damp, dark cave, far from sunshine or warmth. No light. No air. No hope. Alone. Nobody wants to descend into despair.

In Psalm 27 David described being under attack from enemies who assailed him and wanted to eat up his flesh (see v. 2). In verse 13 he was being painfully honest. When he looked at his immediate circumstances, he realized despair would be inevitable if he didn't get help somewhere. He could have and would have been consumed by despair, but he wasn't.

David's transparency encourages us to be honest about even our deepest problems and our most negative feelings. Despair lurks behind various doorways and beneath various trapdoors in life. If our attitude is that it can't happen to us, we are setting ourselves up to be blindsided by the sudden onset of a bleak outlook: *I thought I was headed in the right direction; why do I feel so lost?* Or we get stunned by the severity of a circumstance: *Hey! I knew something like this could happen, but I didn't expect it to be this bad, confusing, and painful.* Or we get immobilized by the quicksand of events that overwhelm us with their finality: *How can it be over? I thought I would have more time or another chance. I don't know what to do now.* Detours into despair are one-way passages that lead to dead ends.

Detours into despair are one-way passages that lead to dead ends.

Have you ever experienced despair?   ☐ Yes   ☐ No

If so, what caused it?

What does despair feel like?

How was your crisis resolved or relieved?

Into the Depths

The dictionary defines *despair* as *destitute of positive expectation.* If you're in despair, you can't see anything good in your future. You have no idea how life could improve. You have no words to pray. You can't return to a better time because the memory or the place is gone. You can't remove the circumstances because the opportunity to make changes has vanished. You can't retrieve the relationship because the person has left. You can't do it over because the time has passed.

David knew the chocking desperation of the cave of despair. His enemies called out to him, "Come down here, David. Go to the bottom. Give it up." In another psalm about his conflicts with adversaries, David said,

> "Reproaches have broken my heart,
> so that I am in despair.
> I looked for pity, but there was none,
> and for comforters, but I found none." *Psalm 69:20*

The Enemy wants nothing more than to destroy a faithful follower of Christ.

He could hear the whispers from the cavern, tempting him to sink into despair. He felt its breath hot on his neck, chasing his hope away. The Enemy wants nothing more than to destroy a faithful follower of Christ. You'll hear that voice too. Learn to recognize it. It will try to call you into the depths of darkness, and although the voice may not seem compelling now, you may come to a place of difficulty where the darkness seems to offer escape. Don't believe it.

What deliberate actions can you take right now to prevent circumstances in your life that might lead you to despair?

Life frequently presents certain accelerants that can push us over the cliff into the cave of despair. Watch out for the following events or crises in your life.

Surprises. These unexpected instances occur when we think life is moving in the right direction, but suddenly an incident, accident, or argument blindsides us. A heart attack. A car accident. A betrayal. Without time to brace ourselves, we can quickly start thinking things will never again be right.

Severity. You probably wouldn't despair over a parking ticket or the breakdown of a television set, but a severe loss delivers an invitation to despair: a professional who loses a cherished career, an athlete who loses mobility, or a teacher who loses the ability to speak. Often severity is brought on by accumulated events that gang up on us, overwhelming our capacity to cope. A classic example can be seen in Job I, when messenger after messenger announced one disaster after another.

Settledness. Despair comes when we believe our misfortune is settled and irreversible. We know certain things will never be the same again. Someone has died. A relationship has ended. A promising opportunity has been lost. These events carry a finality to them that squelches any hopes of resuming life as it was.

> **Despair comes when we believe our misfortune is settled and irreversible.**

Beside each item below, circle the type of accelerant that statement represents.

I have no idea how life can improve	Surprise	Severity	Settledness
I have no words to pray.	Surprise	Severity	Settledness
That came out of nowhere!	Surprise	Severity	Settledness
I can't return to a better time; it's gone.	Surprise	Severity	Settledness
She neglected to mention I would feel this bad.	Surprise	Severity	Settledness
That window of opportunity has vanished.	Surprise	Severity	Settledness
I can't retrieve any level of relationship because the person is gone.	Surprise	Severity	Settledness
Nothing I've tried can fix this.	Surprise	Severity	Settledness

If you are experiencing circumstances that could cause you to despair, check which accelerant is probably bringing it on.

☐ Surprise   ☐ Severity   ☐ Settledness

Picture a blinking, neon warning light here, just inside the opening to the cave of despair. Once we're deep inside, it can be very hard to find our way out. As believers, we have a strategy for avoiding that trap to begin with. God's promises help us guard against the possibility of despair.

The Land of the Living

When you recognize the presence of any of the accelerants we reviewed, persistently negative or unhealthy emotions in your life, or continual thoughts of painful events in the past, please stop. You're headed straight for despair. It's time to look to God's Word before you find yourself overwhelmed. Second Corinthians 10:5 says we are to "take every thought captive to obey Christ." You can choose where you allow your thoughts to go.

Today's Scripture focus shows us the direction David took to avoid being overtaken by despair. These are powerful words of faith:

> "I believe that I shall look upon the goodness of the LORD
> in the land of the living!" *Psalm 27:13*

David not only knew God would eventually sort things out for good in eternity but also had faith that God would work during his lifetime. David believed he would have opportunities to see the goodness of the Lord in this life. A statement like this challenges us to look for evidence of God's goodness all around us, even in the midst of difficult circumstances. God's promises allow us to see His goodness while we are still on this earth.

God's promises allow us to see His goodness while we are still on this earth.

If you are in a situation that is tempting you to despair, what are you doing to be more aware of God's goodness in your life? Check all that apply.

☐ Hoping things will get better
☐ Searching God's Word for hopeful promises
☐ Sliding further into the cave of despair
☐ Believing God's promises of His good intentions for you

David reminds us that our hope must always be placed in the Lord. Deliberately searching out God's promises and believing them by faith will keep our focus on Him and will help us recognize His work in our lives.

During Jesus' final days we see two dramatic examples of despair with two dramatically different endings. Peter boasted that he would never abandon Jesus, but only a few hours later he denied knowing his Master. Judas sold out the Savior for 30 pieces of silver. Both men failed miserably, and both reacted by plummeting into despair. Yet Judas hanged himself, while Peter repented and later experienced Jesus' merciful restoration (see John 21:15-19).

What made the difference? Judas, having sold out to the Evil One, was unable to repent; Jesus called him "the son of destruction" (John 17:12). As badly as Peter failed, he still had a heart for the Lord. He consistently displayed transparency about his shortcomings and a willingness to repent. He waited to see "the goodness of the LORD in the land of the living" (Ps. 27:13). As a result, Peter was among the first to witness the empty tomb and later the risen Christ. His heart was ready to receive restoration when Jesus offered it.

We will lose hope if our eyes are focused anywhere else but on the Lord.

When you feel yourself descending into the cave of despair, look up and grasp the promises of God. Let them lift you up and give you hope. God lives and acts in our world, and He responds to a heart of faith. We will lose hope if our eyes are focused anywhere else but on the Lord. When our eyes are fixed on Him, we will see His goodness.

> **Read again the account of Peter's restoration in John 21:15-19. Put yourself in Peter's place and ask God to show you if there are any specific journeys into despair that He needs to restore in your life as only He can. If He shows you one or more, let Him restore you.**

> **Begin memorizing this week's memory verse, Romans 8:28.**

Day 2

GOD IS ALWAYS GOOD

Today's Scripture Focus

"Be still, and know that I am God.
I will be exalted among the nations,
I will be exalted in the earth!"

Psalm 46:10

Yesterday we saw that David faced the demons of despair and knew how he needed to respond. He heard the tempter's voice telling him to give up, but instead he turned his eyes toward God: "I would have despaired unless I had believed" (Ps. 27:13, NASB). Instead of despairing under assault from his enemies, David chose to believe God. We don't know during what time of his life David wrote this psalm, but any number of external and internal forces in David's experience could have led him toward despair. As a young man he was the runt of the family, overlooked and assigned the menial duties of a shepherd. David was familiar with hostility; his brothers treated him harshly, and later Saul, the king of Israel, persistently tried to kill him. He had friends who turned out to be enemies, and he had enemies who held grudges. He lost several children, partly as a result of parenting problems. And he committed serious sins of his own, breaking some of the Ten Commandments.

Identify two past life experiences that tempted or led you to despair. How did you respond in each situation?

Experience   Response

1.

> Goodness is a constant part of God's character.

2.

Be Still and Know

Even at his lowest David hung on to God's goodness. He realized goodness is a constant part of God's character. It isn't dependent on what we do or don't do. It was something David could place his trust in no matter what the difficult circumstance. He was always able to affirm God's goodness in verses like these:

"Good and upright is the LORD;
therefore he instructs sinners in the way." *Psalm 25:8*

"Oh, taste and see that the LORD is good!
Blessed is the man who takes refuge in him!" *Psalm 34:8*

"You, O Lord, are good and forgiving,
abounding in steadfast love to all who call upon you." *Psalm 86:5*

"The LORD is good;
his steadfast love endures forever,
and his faithfulness to all generations." *Psalm 100:5*

"The LORD is good to all,
and his mercy is over all that he has made." *Psalm 145:9*

We need to take hold of Bible promises that will lead us away from despair and toward steady trust in God's unchanging goodness.

Instead of lighting the match to the accelerants of despair in his life, David fired up his confidence in His promise-keeping God. You and I need to do the same. We need to take hold of Bible promises that will lead us away from despair and toward steady trust in God's unchanging goodness. People sometimes say, "I don't know how she can stay so strong through this." "How can he keep going with everything that's happening?" I'll tell you how to do it: we fix our hope on our promise-keeping God.

Read the following Scripture promises and state how each one can guard you against despair.

"Stand firm, and see the salvation of the LORD. ... The LORD
will fight for you, and you have only to be silent." *Exodus 14:13-14*

"In quietness and in trust shall be your strength." *Isaiah 30:15*

"Be still, and know that I am God." *Psalm 46:10*

God gave Israel the words of Exodus 14:13-14 when the nation, fresh from its escape from slavery, was suddenly stuck between a revenge-driven army and the sea. The people panicked and wanted to backtrack. They asked Moses, "As bad as things were back in Egypt, how could you bring us out here to die by the sword?" Even though God was already reassuring them by His presence in the pillar of cloud and fire, the people looked at the chariot of Egypt and doubted God's goodness. Moses had to tell them the message we need to think about more often when we first encounter a problem of any kind. Your job is to button it up. Don't inflame the situation with stupid talk. Keep your mouth shut and hold on to God's promises. It's all right if you've done everything you can. Now it's time to sit back and watch God work!

Isaiah 30:15 says, "In quietness and in trust shall be your strength." Our helplessness makes God's intervention more obvious. He doesn't need our help! Our job is to trust Him.

Today's Scripture focus, Psalm 46:10, reminds us to "be still, and know that I am God." When we come to the place where we can't do anything else, we must stand still and believe. We think that's the worst possible place to be in our lives, but God loves it when we recognize our dependence on Him. When we can't do it, we need to let God do it all.

God loves it when we recognize our dependence on Him.

David consistently anchored his faith to an unchanging God in the whirlwinds of life. Each time he fell, he boldly reclaimed unflinching faith in God's character and relied on His goodness. David's life was full of end-of-the-rope experiences, and he learned how to hang on when there was nothing else he could do.

> **Identify places in your life where you need to "stand firm, and see the salvation of the Lord" (Ex. 14:13).**

> **What will you do to respond to these challenges in quietness, trust, and reliance on God?**

Eyes to See

In the midst of his crisis, David confessed in Psalm 27:13 (NASB):

> "I would have despaired unless I had believed
> that I would see the goodness of the LORD
> In the land of the living."

Think about the God you're trusting in. Notice the phrase "that I would see." David believed he was going to witness God's work. He wasn't just going to hear about it; he was going to see God's goodness with his own eyes.

Now consider the last phrase in the verse: "in the land of the living." David believed he was going to see God at work during his lifetime. In David's immediate circumstances there may not have been a single compelling reason he could point to and say, "See, there's God's goodness right there. That's why I'm not despairing." The act of faith in the face of despair is to go beyond what we can see to behold the goodness of God. This is a matter of sheer faith. God's goodness gives us permission to visualize the kind of result He can bring about against all odds. Do you have faith to believe like that?

The act of faith in the face of despair is to go beyond what we can see to behold the goodness of God.

Check any circumstances you would like to see resolved in your lifetime.

- ☐ Having your son or daughter come home
- ☐ Seeing your spouse turn back to God
- ☐ Seeing a family member or friend accept Jesus
- ☐ Finding the right spouse
- ☐ Being healed of an illness
- ☐ Having children
- ☐ Experiencing a positive change in your career
- ☐ Other:

The reality is, you may never see a change in your circumstances. The life of faith doesn't know what's going to happen; it simply maintains the perspective that "with God all things are possible" (Matt. 19:26). God calls us to keep our eyes on Him, believing He is good, and that is enough. We will lose hope if our eyes are anywhere but on the Lord. When our eyes are fixed on Him, we see His goodness.

Pray about the issues you marked in which you would like to see God work. Ask Him to give you faith to believe in His goodness and eyes to see Him at work in your life. Ask Him to show you promises in His Word that will help you keep your eyes on Him even if your circumstances never change.

Practice this week's memory verse, Romans 8:28, by writing it here.

Day 3

EXPERIENCING GOD'S GOODNESS

Today's Scripture Focus

"Oh, taste and see that the LORD is good!
Blessed is the man who takes refuge in him!"

Psalm 34:8

Do you know how good God is? Gratefully, each of us could answer, "Not completely, but I'm learning!" We don't know enough about God until we learn that His goodness will always reach beyond our capacity to measure.

Everything God does is for our good. His love is demonstrated in His goodness. Every time God says no, He is exercising the goodness of His mercy. Each time He says yes, it is a good gift. God is good.

Turn to the Ten Commandments in Exodus 20:1-17, a set of nine no commands and one yes command from God. Read the commands and summarize how the no commands express God's mercy.

In what ways is the one yes command a good gift?

The School of Suffering

Our problem is that we tend to have a shortsighted and limited view of God's goodness. When we hear the phrase "God is good," we tend to translate it into "God is good as long as I like everything He does for me. God shows His goodness by making my life easy. I really know He loves me when He keeps anything difficult far away from me!" This approach to God indicates that we misunderstand goodness; it says practically nothing about God.

God loves us too much to limit His great work in our lives to our small and narrow expectations.

God is too good and He loves us too much to limit His great work in our lives to our small and narrow expectations. He's the one who "began a good work in you [and] will bring it to completion at the day of Jesus Christ" (Phil. 1:6).

That's why He enrolls us in the school of suffering. Now that doesn't sound like a school any of us want to attend, but as our parents used to tell us, it's for our own good. Because God created us, He knows what it takes to make us grow in spiritual maturity. Most of the time that won't happen if we are living a life of ease. Even though we may not like it, we can expect a certain amount of suffering in a fallen, sinful world. God's good purposes include His commitment to use all of life's circumstances to bring us to maturity and completeness in Christ.

Read Hebrews 12:5-11 in your Bible and complete this sentence:

God's discipline proves that we are His _____.

Although discipline is painful, what fruit does it yield?

Read James 1:2-4. What should your attitude be when you face trials?

What did James identify as the fruit of trials in a believer's life?

His Goodness Is Our Refuge

A. W. Tozer, a long-time pastor on the south side of Chicago, was no stranger to suffering. Two sons were wounded in World War II. The people in his church turned against him. His own broken health laid him up for weeks at a time. I could go on and on about his sufferings. But his experiences with God's faithfulness flavor everything Tozer wrote. Here are some things Tozer learned from suffering about God's goodness.

God's goodness is something He wants us to experience. Today's Scripture focus, Psalm 34:8, invites us to "taste and see that the LORD is good." When we get a taste of God, we experience something that is infinitely greater than we are. God says, "Taste. Sample and see. Find out for yourself that I am good." He wants us to experience His goodness. He offers Himself to us.

God's goodness is the eventual conclusion of every generation of His children. The psalmist wrote in Psalm 100:5,

"The LORD is good;
his steadfast love endures forever,
and his faithfulness to all generations."

You might not think so now, but if you're one of God's children, you're going to figure it out by the end of your life: God is good. Everything He allows, everything He withholds, every difficult season, every stretching circumstance, He means for your good. His disposition is kindness. His default action is for your benefit. God's goodness flows to us as steadfast love and faithfulness.

God's goodness is evident in everything He does. Psalm 145:9 says,

> "The LORD is good to all,
> and his mercy is over all that he has made."

Even though you may not understand why you are facing despair or difficulty, you can be sure His mercy and kindness permeate what He is doing in your life.

God's goodness may not be immediately obvious. Lamentations 3:25 says, "The LORD is good to those who wait for him." But if you respond to suffering by saying, "I've got to see Your goodness now, God! You've got 10 days to show me You're good, or I'm out of here!" that's not going to work out very well for you. God doesn't respond to bullying. Even His timetable is good, but we can see this only after events have transpired. Our prayer must be "Father, I'm waiting for You because I know You are good in what You do and when You do it."

God's goodness is a refuge, and He is aware of the people who find it. Today's Scripture focus concludes, "Blessed is the man who takes refuge in him!" (Ps. 34:8). Nahum 1:7 says, "The LORD is good, a stronghold in the day of trouble; he knows those who take refuge in him." As God watches us live our lives, He is aware of those who are taking His promises to heart and proving His Word in their lives. He knows the people who are resting in His promises and those who are resisting them. *Stronghold* is what God's goodness looks like to an enemy on the outside; *refuge* is what God's goodness looks like to us on the inside. God draws near in intimate fellowship when we seek protection within His goodness.

God draws near in intimate fellowship when we seek protection within His goodness.

How has past suffering proved an opportunity to grow spiritually and to trust in God's goodness?

If you are suffering now, perhaps dealing with despair, how are you able to see God's goodness in your circumstances?

Are you waiting for God or trying to push Him to get you out of this?

What Scripture promises have you found that give you a taste of God's goodness in your particular situation?

God's promises enable us to "taste and see that the LORD is good!" (Ps. 34:8). Because the Lord's goodness is a refuge, He is aware of those who find it. God Himself is involved directly in His promises; they don't stand apart from Him like a dry but empty storm shelter along the path of life. When we step out of the rain and into His promises, He's right there, acting as our host as we take refuge in Him.

Because the Lord's goodness is a refuge, He is aware of those who find it.

Matthew, Mark, and Luke all include the account of a sick woman who approached Jesus under the cover of a crowd with a simple purpose: "She said to herself, 'If I only touch his garment, I will be made well' " (Matt. 9:21). Two things happened instantly: that woman's condition was taken care of, and "Jesus, perceiving in himself that power had gone out from him, immediately turned about in the crowd and said, 'Who touched my garments?' " (Mark 5:30). He knew someone had just taken refuge in Him! And He wanted her to know that He knew it—and knew her personally.

How can God's promises help you take refuge in God's goodness?

Ask God to show you a Scripture promise that would help you reach out to Him as a refuge in the difficulties or despair you are currently facing. Record the verse here.

Recite and pray your memory verse for this week, Romans 8:28. Praise God for His goodness and express your trust in Him to show you His goodness in any difficult situation you are experiencing. Commit yourself to Him as your refuge in this storm.

TRUSTING GOD'S PLAN

Today's Scripture Focus

"I know the plans I have for you, declares the Lord, plans
for welfare and not for evil, to give you a future and a hope."
Jeremiah 29:11

God's goodness isn't hidden or buried. It is relentless. God wants us to experience His goodness. He's not interested in our saying, "God is good" as a cheer to stir up the team. He wants us to finish that statement in concrete ways: "God is good, and I can't wait to tell you how He's shown His goodness lately!" The assertion that God is good is of little use as a theological slogan, but it is life itself when we know with every fiber of our being that it's true.

Today's Scripture focus states that our good God has good, specific plans for our lives—and He knows what they are. He's not making things up as He goes along. There's no danger that God's plans will somehow go awry and He will have to punt. God knows. The problem for us is, we don't know. And we want to know. And when we tell God that, He responds with, "No, I'm not going to give you the details, but I'll give you the broad strokes."

Why do you think God doesn't give us all of the details about His plans for us ahead of time?

God has a plan for your life that He's working out. You may get stuck in the bottomless vortex of *Whom should I marry? Where will I live? What should I major in? What about a job?* You want to know specifics. But God's plans are not so much about those details as they are about developing your character and installing in you the wisdom and righteousness you need to walk with Him by faith. How much would you depend on Him if you already knew the answer to everything? More than the questions about specifics, God wants you to focus on *Who am I? Who is God? What is my purpose in life? What does God want me to do?* God gives you the information you need to take the next step of faith with Him. If you believe He is good and is working out your life for your good, you don't need to know all of the details now.

> God's goodness
> isn't hidden or buried.
> It is relentless.

- [ ] I need to know more information now.
- [ ] I am confident that God is working this out for my good.
- [ ] I will trust God for my needs today.
- [ ] I have difficulty believing God can make this right.
- [ ] Other:

A Future and a Hope

Today's Scripture focus is one of the greatest promises in the Bible: "I know the plans I have for you, declares the LORD, plans for welfare and not for evil, to give you a future and a hope" (Jer. 29:11). When God instructed Jeremiah to write these words, the nation of Israel was in exile in a foreign country. Everything around the people was unfamiliar, and their departing memories of the promised land were pictures of utter devastation. There wasn't much to go back to except the broken walls of Jerusalem and the ruins of the once glorious temple. Yet when they were far from home in captivity, God drew near to them and said, "This isn't going to change right away. You're going to be here for a while, but I have not left you alone. I have plans for your welfare and your future that will give you hope. Wait on Me."

We may not have all of the details about God's plan for us, but this verse gives us important clues about what He desires.

A plan for our welfare. The Hebrew word for *welfare* is *shalom,* a complete state of well-being, fulfillment, prosperity, and peace. God's plans are for your total well-being. Sure, you can mess things up a bit if you insist on doing things your own way, but you'll never derail His plans. Remember that God's purpose for you may not include—and is a lot bigger than—easy circumstances, material wealth, and success in your career. His concern is your relationship with Him, a relationship of love, trust, and obedience that brings you every spiritual blessing through Jesus Christ. Such a relationship may come only after your faith has been purified and refined through the fires of adversity. This is why many people in very difficult circumstances can face each day in the joy of the Lord. Even if things around them don't seem to be going so well, it is well with their souls.

A plan that is not for evil. God's plans are definitely not for evil. They are worked out for our good in a creation permeated by evil, and we are deeply affected by evil in the process, but His plans are for good. If you are giving in to sin, that is not God's plan for your life, and it will eventually lead you right into the pit of

You can mess things up a bit if you insist on doing things your own way, but you'll never derail God's plans.

despair. People who are determined to live at cross-purposes with God's plan pay a high price for their experiment. Our plans take us right into the middle of sin; they never work out for good. God's plans take us away from evil and into the good He wants to give us.

A future. God's plans also hold out a future for you—on earth and in eternity. Things might not look that great on the horizon right now, but God sees way beyond the horizon of our earthbound view. His perspective is eternal, and He is in charge of that. If you place your life in His hands by faith, you can rest in His plans for your short-term and long-term welfare.

A hope. God's plans for you are ones you can look forward to. They give you hope, a confident expectation of something better tomorrow. If your confidence is in what you and other humans can deliver, you will always be disappointed in life. God, on the other hand, always delivers on His plans. If you keep your eyes on the Lord, you will always have hope.

> **Think about a trial you are in that could lead to despair. State how each component of God's promise in Jeremiah 29:11 helps you trust God's plan for your life as He brings you through this difficult situation.**

A plan for your welfare:

A plan that is not for evil:

A future:

A hope:

Enjoying God's Goodness

One problem we encounter when we face hardship is that, being the earthbound creatures we are, we become completely absorbed in our circumstances and forget that God is still there working for our good. Promises like Jeremiah 29:11 remind us that He remains ready and willing to work His good plan for our lives if we acknowledge His goodness, turn this trial over to Him, and submit

Things might not look that great on the horizon right now, but God sees way beyond the horizon.

to His larger purposes for our lives. When you stand at the entrance to the cave of despair and feel that downward tug, it's time to get your heart and thoughts focused on God's goodness. That's what God's promises can do for you. And if you learn these promises now, you will be ready to look to your Good Shepherd when despair tries to drag you down.

Let's look at some promises that can help us enjoy God's goodness.

"The LORD is good;
his steadfast love endures forever,
and his faithfulness to all generations." *Psalm 100:5*

Are you leaving a legacy of faith to your children or the children of others? Today find a way to share a promise of God's goodness with the next generation.

"The LORD is good to all,
and his mercy is over all that he has made." *Psalm 145:9*

How are you enjoying evidence of God's goodness today?

Enjoying God's goodness is the best way to stay out of the cave of despair.

"The LORD is good to those who wait for him,
to the soul who seeks him." *Lamentations 3:25*

Are you reading God's Word every day as a way of seeking His promises for your life? If not, will you make a commitment to do that?

Set your mind on enjoying God's goodness every day. Revel in His promises that He is good and has good plans for you. Look for ways He is expressing His goodness toward you, even in the midst of your trials and the stress of your day. Share the blessings of His goodness with others. Enjoying God's goodness is the best way to stay out of the cave of despair.

Practice reciting this week's memory verse, Romans 8:28.

IT'S ALL FOR GOOD

Today's Scripture Focus

"We know that for those who love God all things work together
for good, for those who are called according to his purpose."

Romans 8:28

Today's Scripture focus has been a perennial favorite among believers, for it is a promise clearly written for those who are involved in a love relationship with God. It's very easy for us to paraphrase this verse and end up with the wrong idea that only good things happen to those who love God. Unfortunately, in "all things" there are plenty of hard things. But the consistent testimony of generations of believers is that the more they go through, the more they love God. If we respond to hardship by loving God and placing our faith in Him, "all things work together for good."

Through the years I've come to understand that when you're suffering, your nose is up against a brick wall, and you can't see anything but hard and red. All of the things you can see at that point may not look good. In those moments you can hardly recognize God's goodness. As the years go by and you take a step backward and then another and another, you get more time and separation from your circumstances, and you begin to make out the mural that is painted on the wall. Eventually, you can see that your pain was part of a much larger picture that God was painstakingly creating.

> **Eventually, you can see that your pain was part of a much larger picture that God was painstakingly creating.**

Describe a painful situation in your past in which God worked for your good.

What Scripture promise have you learned in this study that has helped you see God's larger picture for your life, one you never noticed before?

We Know

Yesterday we admitted our frustration with not knowing God's plans for our lives, but we found comfort in the fact that God knows those plans, and we can trust Him with them. Romans 8:28 tells us something else we can know: "We know that for those who love God all things work together for good, for those who are called according to his purpose." We don't merely think God is working for our good. We don't merely wonder. We know. The word *know* communicates experiential knowledge—the kind that comes from life. You didn't go to church or to college to have this explained to you. You didn't Google the answer. You know because you've been through it. This is one of those tried-and-true promises in God's Word about the way God works.

List ways believers can know God always works for good in their lives.

Those Who Love God

Notice that the promise of Romans 8:28 applies only to those who love God. That requirement can be daunting if we think we have to generate in ourselves some kind of strong attraction to God that will impress Him with its intensity. That's not going to happen. Yet Jesus said loving God is the central command of Scripture: "The most important is, Hear, O Israel: The Lord our God, the Lord is one. And you shall love the Lord your God with all your heart and with all your soul and with all your mind and with all your strength" (Mark 12:29-30). By commanding us to love God, Jesus didn't mean we have to love Him perfectly. That's not in us. But we can learn to love God increasingly.

> We can learn to love God increasingly.

Identify three times in your life when your love for God increased noticeably.

1.

2.

3.

Next to each occasion listed above, identify the reason your love for God grew as something you did or something God did.

If our love for God has to originate with us, we know it's not going far. Then where does our love for God come from? Read I John 4:15-19:

"Whoever confesses that Jesus is the Son of God, God abides in him,
and he in God. So we have come to know and to believe the love that
God has for us. God is love, and whoever abides in love abides in God,
and God abides in him. By this is love perfected with us, so that we may
have confidence for the day of judgment, because as he is so also are we
in this world. There is no fear in love, but perfect love casts out fear.
For fear has to do with punishment, and whoever fears has not
been perfected in love. We love because he first loved us."

We're not the source of love—any love. At our best we are reflectors and channels of God's love. He is the source. Even when we want to obey the Great Commandment, we're just giving back to God what He first gave to us. We can depend on Him to keep His promises, not because of something we do but because He loves us and gives us the capacity to love Him.

Some of us have difficulty loving God because we have had human relationships that failed, and we ended up being deeply hurt. Don't let an imperfect relationship distort your understanding of God's love. He says, "I have loved you with an everlasting love" (Jer. 31:3). Unlike human love, God's love never fails and never ends. He gave His Son to redeem us from sin so that we could enjoy an eternal love relationship with Him. No disappointment on this earth can get in the way of that.

> **Unlike human love, God's love never fails and never ends.**

If a past relationship is making it hard for you to love God, place that relationship in His hands. Ask Him to show you Scripture promises that reveal His love for you. Here are some you can begin with: Psalm 26:3; 33:5; 147:11; John 3:16; Romans 8:38-39; 1 John 3:1; 4:19. Ask Him to fill your heart with His love and to free you to love Him with all your heart, soul, mind, and strength.

Those Who Are Called

Romans 8:28 indicates that only God's children—those who have turned from their sin and embraced Christ by faith, those who are increasingly learning how to love God more and more—understand the great promise of this verse. That's what it means to be "called according to his purpose." Ephesians 1:5 says, "He predestined us for adoption as sons through Jesus Christ, according to the purpose of his will."

Explain in your own words what you think it means to be called according to God's purpose.

Why can only believers claim the promise that God will work all things for their good?

Faith in God is required to see Him work. Only those who belong to God can test His promises and prove His faithful love as He brings about His purpose for their lives. And what is God's ultimate purpose for His children? It's found in the next verse: "Those whom he foreknew he also predestined to be conformed to the image of his Son" (Rom. 8:29). From eternity God planned to call a people for Himself who would become like His Son, Jesus, through rebirth and spiritual growth. His purpose is nothing less than to transform you into the image of His Son by renewing your mind, reorienting your priorities, reshaping your character, revising your life purpose, and redirecting your destiny. When God works all things for our good, He has that grand and glorious goal in mind.

Working All Things Together

Romans 8:28 says if we love God and are called according to His purpose, "all things work together for good." "All things" means *all* things, not just the pleasurable things. It includes our trials, our problems, our despair, our suffering. As humans, we all experience these things, not because God causes them but because they are part of life in a world that is immersed in sin.

List current circumstances in your life and categorize them as good or bad from an earthly perspective. Select specific issues from general areas like health, career, family, church, and so on.

Good	Bad

If you love God and trust that He is always good, you will submit to Him as He works through your trial.

From God's perspective it doesn't matter what the circumstance is. He has promised in His Word that He will take whatever you are dealing with and use it for your good. Your good may not look like what you would choose. You may not get the job or the spouse or the salary or the good health you want while you are on this earth. But if you love God and trust that He is always good, you will submit to Him as He works through your trial. You will place your life in His hands and ask Him to mold you in the image of His Son. You will believe His promise to bring your ultimate good from this situation.

Choose one of the things you categorized as bad in the previous activity and try to view it from an eternal perspective. State how you think God can bring good from this situation.

Have life's difficulties caught you off guard? Do you wonder whether God is good? If He wasn't going to use that hardship for your good, it wouldn't have happened. He had to sign off on every single thing that touches your life. He's sovereign, remember? If He let it happen, He's going to use it for good. He's not the cause of evil, but He's the solution. As the master chess player, He takes every move we make and strategizes to ensure that His purposes are accomplished.

Read the following Scriptures and identify what each one promises for those who let God transform them through their trials.

Philippians 3:8-9:

Hebrews 4:16:

Hebrews 12:5-6:

James 1:2-4:

James 1:12:

The ultimate good of Romans 8:28 is not your little blueprint for your life; the ultimate good is God's blueprint for the universe and your place in it. Are you committed to God's purposes? Do you want His will to be fulfilled and His kingdom to advance? Do you want to be a part of His grand plan? Submitting to God's purpose means we understand that this is not about us; it's about God.

> Submitting to God's purpose means we understand that this is not about us; it's about God.

Check any of God's greater purposes that you feel your trials are preventing you from participating in.

- ☐ Witnessing
- ☐ Ministering to others
- ☐ Church involvement
- ☐ Other:
- ☐ Making disciples
- ☐ Making friends
- ☐ Daily Bible study and prayer

Pray about any trials that are still tempting you to despair. Recite your memory verse for this week, Romans 8:28. Claim this verse as God's promise that He will work this out for your good. Ask Him to refocus your attention and energy on joining His purposes for you and for His kingdom.

Week 5

I WILL NOT FALTER
GOD IS ALWAYS
WATCHING

This Week's Promise

I will not fear; God is always with me.

I will not doubt; God is always in control.

I will not despair; God is always good.

I WILL NOT FALTER; GOD IS ALWAYS WATCHING.

I will not fail; God is always victorious.

This Week's Memory Verse

"No temptation has overtaken you that is not common to man. God is faithful, and he will not let you be tempted beyond your ability, but with the temptation he will also provide the way of escape, that you may be able to endure it." *1 Corinthians 10:13*

On the Fence

When you think about Scotland, you might think about the lochs, or lakes. There are more than 20,000 of them, and the largest is the famous Loch Ness. Even more impressive than the lochs are the Scottish Highlands, massive green hills that tower over the northern part of the country. The highest, Ben Nevis, is almost five thousand feet high. My family and I went there a few years ago to rest and spend time with God, and when I saw the highlands, I was reminded of Psalm 147:8:

> "He covers the heavens with clouds;
> he prepares rain for the earth;
> he makes grass grow on the hills."

That was a time in my family's life when we were in danger of faltering. We greatly needed spiritual perspective and renewal, and there on those lush hills of Scotland, we found that God saw our need. Just as God is faithful to water the Scottish hills and make the grass grow, He was faithful to bring us to a point of renewed commitment to Him as the number one priority in our lives.

One of the rare places where the Bible uses the term *falter* can be found in Elijah's confrontation of the Israelites before he threw down the gauntlet for a sacrifice-off with the pagan gods. Elijah had already invited Ahab to send the pagan A-team to Mount Carmel: "Ahab sent for all the children of Israel, and gathered the prophets together on Mount Carmel. And Elijah came to all the people, and said, 'How long will you falter between two opinions? If the Lord is God, follow Him; but if Baal, follow him.' But the people answered him not a word" (1 Kings 18:20-21, NKJV).

Clearly, the people of Israel were on the fence about whom they would worship, unable to make up their minds. They had a history of God's amazing faithfulness to them as a people on the one hand and all the tantalizing, tempting debauchery of pagan worship on the other. The Israelites were faltering between two belief systems. As Elijah stood there seething, the people responded with sullen silence.

Has your trial brought you to a place where you might falter? Maybe you think God isn't aware of your issue, and you feel you are going to be crushed under the weight of your burden. God's Word records that God was watching His people in Elijah's day, and He's watching now. He didn't want His people to falter then, and He doesn't want you to falter now. There's a purpose in His watching, and it's for your good!

Week 5

GROUP EXPERIENCE

On the Same Page

1. Relate humorous or absurd observations you have heard other parents make during children's athletic events.

2. Share a time when positive words of encouragement prevented you from faltering during difficulty.

Preparation and Review

1. Practice reciting the previous weeks' memory verses.

2. Together read aloud this week's memory verse on page 108.

3. What does the word *falter* mean? What problems can result when believers falter in their faith?

DVD Session 5 Viewer Guide

Daniel
3:24

Shadrach,
Meshach +
Bendigo

Promise 4: I will not _____; God is _____.

"Fear not, for I have _____ you" (Isa. 43:1).

Redemption: the Lord comes with the wealth of His riches and buys me out of the slavery of _____ and makes me _____ _____.

"I have called you by name, you are _____" (Isa. 43:1).
"When you pass through the waters, I will be _with_ you" (Isa. 43:2).
"... and through the rivers, they shall not _____ you" (Isa. 43:2).

You're not going to _____ _____ (see Isa. 43:2).

"When you walk through fire you shall not be _alone_" (Isa. 43:2).
"The flame shall not _consume_ you" (Isa. 43:2).

I will not falter; God is _watching_.

Wrong views of God's watching:

1. A resentful _relative_   Zephania 3:17
2. A _hawk_   Psalm 103:14
3. A crabby _church_ _lady_
4. A suspicious _parent_
5. A cantankerous _boss_

The eyes of the Lord:

1. Are _inescapable_   Proverbs 15:3
2. Are synonymous with what is _right_ and _true_   Deuteronomy 13:18
3. Are focused upon and attentive to _His_ _own_   1 Peter 3:12
4. Are searching for people to _bless_   2 Chronicles 16:9
5. Are provoked to _grace_ when He observes a righteous person   Genesis 6:8

      Philippians 4:13

God "will not let you be tempted beyond your _ability_ " (1 Cor. 10:13). "With the temptation or trial he will also provide the way of _escape_ " (1 Cor. 10:13).

Ways of escape:

1. God will take you _out_ of the trial.
2. God will send you _encouragement_ to persevere.
3. God will give you _wisdom_ to act.   James 1:5
4. God will give you _strength_ to persevere.
5. God will send _someone_ to help you bear the burden.
6. God will give you _relief_ .

Responding to the DVD Teaching

1. **If faltering in the Christian life means constantly taking steps backward and forward, never settling into a deliberate and sustained direction of growth, how have you exhibited this pattern in your spiritual life?**

2. **How does God's watching, as described in this video session, differ from the way you have thought about it before?**

3. **How do you think your awareness that God is watching going to affect the way you live this week?**

Read week 5 and complete the activities before the next group experience. Read and recite this week's memory verse, 1 Corinthians 10:13, at least once each day this week.

This video session is available for download at *www.lifeway.com/alwaystrue.*

REDEEMED NOT TO FALTER

Today's Scripture Focus

"Thus says the LORD,
he who created you, O Jacob,
he who formed you, O Israel:
'Fear not, for I have redeemed you;
I have called you by name, you are mine.
When you pass through the waters, I will be with you;
and through the rivers, they shall not overwhelm you;
when you walk through fire you shall not be burned,
and the flame shall not consume you.' "

Isaiah 43:1-2

In the film *Chariots of Fire*, about the early life of missionary hero Eric Liddell, there is an amazing scene during a race when he stumbles and falls. The field sprints on, and the camera switches to slow motion as Eric rolls, rises, and rushes back onto the track. Behind but not out, Eric surges back into the race, closing on runner after runner until he crosses the finish line in victory. He faltered, but he didn't give up. His faltering led to the opportunity for an amazing comeback.

What are signs of faltering in the Christian life? Check any options that apply.

- ☐ Neglecting prayer and God's Word
- ☐ Failing to worship God and give Him glory
- ☐ Allowing yourself to sin
- ☐ Doing things in your own strength instead of relying on God
- ☐ Focusing on the things of the world instead of on God
- ☐ Other:

Faltering in your Christian walk means you have moved away from God and are not walking in faith.

Faltering in the Christian life might include any of these behaviors. We've talked about fear, doubt, and moments of despair. Faltering is more serious. When you falter, you are overwhelmed by a severe problem that isn't going to get better in a couple of days or even weeks. Faltering in your Christian walk means you have moved away from God and are not walking in faith. Yet when you falter, you are down but not out. You can suffer setbacks in your Christian life, but God redeemed you so that you would not stay back. You can falter temporarily, but you don't want this to become a permanent pattern.

Through the Fire

God promises if you're walking by faith and embracing His promises for your life, you're not going to falter and stay down. You're not only going to keep moving in God's direction, but you're also going to go through whatever blocks your path—come fire or high water.

Isaiah 43:1-2, today's Scripture focus, is one of the most treasured promises for God's children in all of His Word.

Reread today's Scripture focus on page 112. What do you think water and fire represent in our walk with God?

If we are going to make this promise our own, we have to understand the setting. The preceding chapter, Isaiah 42, indicates that God was in the process of judging His people. They had become wayward and rebellious, disloyal to the one true God and indulging in idolatry:

> "They are turned back and utterly put to shame,
>   who trust in carved idols,
>   who say to metal images,
> 'You are our gods.' " *Isaiah 42:17*

Disgusted by Israel's sin, God was placing some heavy consequences on their actions. If you look at the whole chapter, you see example after example of their failure and the resulting fallout as God allowed them to experience the consequences of paganism and disobedience He had warned them about since the days of Moses (see Deut. 10–11; 13:6-18). Finally, in Isaiah 42:25 the prophet identified who was behind their current troubles—God Himself:

> "He poured on him the heat of his anger
>   and the might of battle;
> it set him on fire all around, but he did not understand;
>   it burned him up, but he did not take it to heart."

God admitted, "I piled all this on you, and you're still not getting it." The rising waters and raging fires described here and in chapter 43 represented the consequences of the nation's sin. God brought the nation through these trials to make them recognize their sin and the urgent need to repent, but sadly, they remained blind to the purpose of His discipline.

God promises if you're walking by faith and embracing His promises for your life, you're not going to falter and stay down.

Think about a time when you faltered in your faith and indulged in sin. What do you think caused you to falter?

What consequences did God allow in your life to bring you to a point of repentance?

I Have Redeemed You

The harsh reality described in Isaiah 42 forms the background for the comfort that begins in Isaiah 43:1:

> "Thus says the LORD,
> he who created you, O Jacob,
> he who formed you, O Israel:
> 'Fear not, for I have redeemed you;
> I have called you by name, you are mine.'"

Through Isaiah, God reminded His people that He had redeemed them. This message immediately connected the current generation of Israel with their ancestors who left Egypt. The idea of redemption had been a central theme in the lives of God's chosen people as they suffered in Egyptian bondage. God had promised, "I am the LORD, and I will bring you out from under the burdens of the Egyptians, and I will deliver you from slavery to them, and I will redeem you with an outstretched arm and with great acts of judgment" (Ex. 6:6). Once God had brought His people out of slavery, He explained to them that redemption had cost the firstborn sons and animals of Egypt (see Ex. 13:11-16). From then on, God would own every firstborn Israelite son or animal. In the case of the animals, with the exception of donkeys, the firstborn was sacrificed to God. In the case of firstborn sons, God would redeem: He would allow them to live even though their lives belonged to Him. Redemption is the forgiveness of a debt made possible because another party has covered the cost.

Redemption is the forgiveness of a debt made possible because another party has covered the cost.

How does God's redemptive work in Israel's history provide a backdrop for understanding the redemption Jesus provided on the cross?

God's redemptive acts throughout Israel's history created a vocabulary and pictures to help His people understand what God was going to accomplish through His Son on the cross. Hebrews 9:22 makes the connection for us: "Under the law almost everything is purified with blood, and without the shedding of blood there is no forgiveness of sins." The apostle Paul pointed out that redemption means we are owned by Someone: "You are not your own, for you were bought with a price. So glorify God in your body" (I Cor. 6:19-20). Because Christ redeemed us, He owns us.

Reread Isaiah 43:1 on page 114 and apply it personally. What does Christ's ownership mean for your Christian walk?

When we say we belong to Christ, it's more than having a name like Christian; it's having a new life that is no longer ours to use as we see fit. Our experience with sin shows that our way doesn't work. We express Christ's ownership by dying to our old way of life and by letting Him live His life through us.

The same was true of the relationship between God and Israel. Although the people had badly faltered and now found themselves in a desperate situation, God reminded them that He had redeemed them and that they belonged to Him. Then He gave them this great and precious promise:

> "When you pass through the waters, I will be with you;
> and through the rivers, they shall not overwhelm you;
> when you walk through fire you shall not be burned,
> and the flame shall not consume you." *Isaiah 43:2*

In spite of Israel's disloyalty to their Redeemer, God promised that He would be with them through the trials that had resulted from their rebellion. The waters might get deep, but they wouldn't get too deep. God would be with them, and His people would get through this difficult and trying time.

Too many times we look for ways to get around deep waters and dangerous fires rather than through them. That's sheer futility. If God has allowed you to go through a trial, He has a purpose for it, and that's where you'll find Him at work. He leads us into difficult seasons, but He brings us through them. You're not going under. You're not going to be swept away. You'll get through this because God is watching, and He will be with you.

If God has allowed you to go through a trial, He has a purpose for it, and that's where you'll find Him at work.

Identify a time when you experienced a trial and tried to escape it rather than let God carry you through it. Or identify a time when you submitted to God's transforming work as you went through a trial. Tell what you learned through either experience.

If your faith is faltering now, note some ways you have moved away from intimate fellowship with God.

Reclaim the truth that Jesus has redeemed you.

Talk to God about your situation. Reclaim the truth that Jesus has redeemed you. Praise Him for giving His life for you. Ask Him to forgive you and to bring you through this time as He has promised.

Begin working on your memory verse for this week, 1 Corinthians 10:13.

THE ATTENTIVE GOD

Today's Scripture Focus

"Our God whom we serve is able to deliver us from the burning fiery furnace, and he will deliver us out of your hand, O king."

Daniel 3:17

After rebelling against God and reaping God's discipline, the nation of Israel never fully learned its lesson and found itself increasingly suffering under the sword of God's judgment. The northern kingdom of Israel was conquered by the Assyrians and carried into exile in 722 B.C. When the southern kingdom of Judah also came under God's judgment and was carried off to Babylon in 587 B.C., Daniel and his friends were among the Hebrew captives. Their dramatic story is told in the Book of Daniel. Fortunately, the men were chosen to be trained for service in King Nebuchadnezzar's court. From the start they decided they would not defile themselves with the king's food or wine but would remain faithful to God. For a while everything went smoothly, and the young men found favor in the king's court.

> The nation of Israel never fully learned its lesson and found itself increasingly suffering under the sword of God's judgment.

When Fires Come

Daniel 3 introduces a slight complication in the story. That chapter begins with a description of a huge image King Nebuchadnezzar had erected. He passed a law that stated when the signal was given, everyone had to bow in worship before the statue or be ushered into a furnace of blazing fire. Bow or burn was the slogan of the day. So when the horn sounded and the multitude hit the deck, the three guys who remained on their feet stood out.

Daniel's best friends had been set up (see Dan. 3:8-12). We're not sure where Daniel was during this incident. It appears this was a provincial matter limited to the area right around Babylon, and Daniel may have had duties elsewhere in the sprawling kingdom. The account drips with political intrigue. Shadrach, Meshach, and Abednego held the highest offices in that province, and there were people who wanted to remove them from power. So when they were reported to the king, things got tense in a hurry.

During the encounter that followed, the king asked, "Who is the god who will deliver you out of my hands?" (v. 15). The men were resolute: "Our God whom we serve is able to deliver us from the burning fiery furnace, and he will deliver us out of your hand, O king. But if not, be it known to you, O king, that we will not serve your gods or worship the golden image that you have set up" (vv. 17-18). Notice they didn't try to take credit for what God could do. They placed their full confidence in the fact that He was able. And even if they didn't get out of this alive, they would still be delivered into God's hands. Either way they would not serve false gods or worship the statue.

Believers today are under increasing pressure to compromise and hide their faith in Christ. Give some examples you know about.

These men did not falter, because they were certain of one thing: they were not going to worship anything other than the one true God, even if they had to give up their lives.

How does any kind of trial tempt believers to falter in their faith?

How would God's promise to be with you through trials give you courage not to falter?

These men did not falter, because they were certain of one thing: they were not going to worship anything other than the one true God, even if they had to give up their lives. Needless to say, the king got hot, and the showdown was set.

God Is There

King Nebuchadnezzar, filled with rage, ordered the furnace heated seven times hotter than usual, and had the three men cast in. Just when we think our boys are toast, look what happened next: "King Nebuchadnezzar was astonished and rose up in haste. He declared to his counselors, 'Did we not cast three men bound into the fire? ... But I see four men unbound, walking in the midst of the fire, and they are not hurt; and the appearance of the fourth is like a son of the gods' " (Dan. 3:24-25). This is an awesome scene. Jesus Christ, the preincarnate second person of the Trinity, was with them, just as He had promised.

Astonished, to say the least, Nebuchadnezzar had the men hauled out of the furnace. Then "the satraps, the prefects, the governors, and the king's counselors gathered together and saw that the fire had not had any power over the bodies of those men. The hair of their heads was not singed, their cloaks were not harmed, and no smell of fire had come upon them. Nebuchadnezzar answered and said, 'Blessed be the God of Shadrach, Meshach, and Abednego, who has sent his angel and delivered his servants, who trusted in him' " (vv. 27-28). Because the three men had given credit to God ahead of time, there was no mystery about who had delivered them from the hand of the wicked king.

God proved that His earlier promise in Isaiah 43:2 was not only for the nation of Israel but also for each of His children. He walked through the fire with Shadrach, Meshach, and Abednego, and they were not burned. The same is true for us today. Your trial might get hot, but it's not going to get too hot. Your Father promises that you're not going to get burned.

Scripture offers many examples showing that God watches His children. Read the following passages and record the ways God observed.

Genesis 6:11-13:

Exodus 3:7-8:

Numbers 6:24-26:

Psalm 141:3:

What trial or problem are you experiencing that is pressuring you to falter in your faith?

You can believe God sees you. He's not missing a single detail in your life. He hears your conversations with your spouse. He sees your checkbook. He knows your unspoken fears. He sees when your faith starts to falter. He's also watching the depth of the water. He's monitoring the heat of the fire. He's pouring out the strength you need to endure when you feel you can't go on. At this moment God is watching your life, and at some point in this trial He will say, "Enough."

You may never have to face a fiery furnace, but as you try to remain true to Christ, you will face other obstacles and challenges that seem just as intimidating. It's not the brand of the furnace that matters; it's whether you're willing to trust God to take you through it, no matter what happens. You don't need to falter. God promises that He is watching.

> It's not the brand of the furnace that matters; it's whether you're willing to trust God to take you through it, no matter what happens.

Do you need to take a stand on one of God's promises? Use one of the verses you read today to express your faith in God's presence with you in your trial.

Practice saying this week's memory verse, 1 Corinthians 10:13.

Day 3

GOD WATCHES

Today's Scripture Focus

"He knows our frame;
he remembers that we are dust."
Psalm 103:14

God knows everything about you. The Bible teaches that He is omnipresent; He is everywhere throughout His creation. He is also omniscient; He knows everything about all He created. David affirmed these ideas in the opening lines of a psalm that is a favorite of many believers:

"O LORD, you have searched me and known me!
You know when I sit down and when I rise up;
you discern my thoughts from afar.
You search out my path and my lying down
and are acquainted with all my ways."
Psalm 139:1-3

Look at the verbs David used to describe God's omniscience: God searched, knew, discerned, and was acquainted with David's thoughts and actions. David had no doubt that God was watching him and was intimately involved in his life.

Created for a Purpose

God also knows us by virtue of having created us. According to today's Scripture focus, God "knows our frame" (Ps. 103:14). Because He created us, He's got all of the specs on the tip of His tongue. He engineered our design with certain capabilities and purposes in mind. He decided which components of our model would be standard and what special features He would include in each of us. He was on the assembly line the day you were put together. As David expressed it so intimately,

God engineered our design with certain capabilities and purposes in mind.

"You formed my inward parts;
you knitted me together in my mother's womb."
Psalm 139:13

Check any statements that describe your reaction to the fact that God created you with specific purposes in mind.

☐ God has graciously shown me the purpose He in had in mind for my life.
☐ God must have made a mistake. I have no idea what I'm doing here.
☐ I am thankful God is revealing His purpose for me even when I get off track.
☐ I know God is watching me and is working out His purpose for me.
☐ Other:

There's one little expression that was never heard in God's assembly room when He put each of us together—"Oops!" He didn't make any mistakes. God created each of us with a purpose, and He doesn't forget what He had in mind. His purpose doesn't change. He "knows our frame" (Ps. 103:14). He's not going to ask us to be something totally different from His loving, specific design for us.

Verse 14 also says God "remembers that we are dust." We're pretty much mud. Break our bodies down to the basic components, and it's not all that impressive a collection of minerals and chemicals in water. Look at the way we were originally made: "The Lord God formed the man of dust from the ground and breathed into his nostrils the breath of life, and the man became a living creature" (Gen. 2:7). When God is watching you and me, He never forgets exactly who we are and the purposes He created us for. At the same time, He remembers that we are frail human beings who sin and falter.

> When God is watching you and me, He never forgets exactly who we are and the purposes He created us for.

What do you think some of the design specs were that God used to create you for His specific purposes?

Identify ways God has used your specific gifts and abilities in His kingdom.

If you are struggling in an area of your life or faltering in your faith, how does it make you feel to know that God remembers you are dust?

God's Way of Watching

When we picture God watching us, many people misunderstand or even suspect His purposes. Following are several wrong views of the way God watches us.

God doesn't watch us like a resentful parent. Some people think God's job is to point out our mistakes and to keep us from having a good time, so He is watching to make sure nothing good happens to us. But Zephaniah 3:17 says,

> "The LORD ... will rejoice over you with gladness; ...
> he will exult over you with loud singing."

God is out for your happiness. He's at the front of the balcony cheering on every good thing that happens in your life. Every wise decision you make, every righteous action you take, God is yelling, "Good for you!" He's on your side.

God doesn't watch us like a hawk on the hunt. Some people view God way up there, cruising at 10,000 feet, spying you out. He's just waiting for you to falter and then—gotcha! He swoops down to grab you by the neck at your first wrong thought or action. Step out of line, and you'll get zapped. But God's not like that. Romans 8:1 makes this great promise: "There is therefore now no condemnation for those who are in Christ Jesus." He gave you His Son to save you from the condemnation of sin, and you became His child. Psalm 103:14 assures us, "He remembers that we are dust." God knows the challenges you face. He has given you His Spirit and His Word—everything you need for victory. He doesn't want you to fail. Because He loves you, He wants to bless you and fill your life with good things. Trusting in God's promises leads to bold living, not fear.

God doesn't watch us like our worst critic. No matter what you do, there's always that one person whose approval you will never earn. Many people view God as being like that judgmental person who is never happy with the choices you make. Psalm 31:8 says, "You have set my feet in a broad place." You're not in danger of falling off the ledge with God. If your heart is fully His and you make choices that honor Him, He will be pleased with you.

God doesn't watch us like a cantankerous boss. Many people imagine hearing God say, "Aren't you over your little trial yet? Do what I tell you and stop wasting My time. Get back to work! Serve Me more and get over yourself." That's not the way it goes with God at all. When He watches you, it is with the most loving, gracious, kind, benevolent interest in your well-being.

At Harvest Bible Chapel we have services when the kids' choirs sing. They come dressed in all their finery, and their parents literally fall all over themselves to get their kids' pictures. Every note and nuance is captured on video. As far as they're concerned, their kid is the only one on the stage. These loving parents' eyes are glued to their little ones with teary-eyed pride and joy. God loves you like that.

Every wise decision you make, every righteous action you take, God is yelling, "Good for you!"

Go back and place check marks beside any ways you have misunderstood God's watching in the past.

Read Psalm 37:4-7 in your Bible. Check the truths these verses teach about the way God regards your life.

- [ ] God will grant your heart's desires if you delight in Him.
- [ ] God will act if you commit your way to Him.
- [ ] God wants to bless you and make you righteous.
- [ ] Try to please other people, and you will please God.
- [ ] Your job is to wait on the Lord.

Don't let fallible humans cause you to misunderstand the wonderful truth that God is watching for your blessing and benefit. God's Word makes it clear that He watches over us not to pick up on the first hint that we may be faltering; He watches over us in order to help us not falter. God is very clear about His motivation for watching: He loves us, and His purposes for us are always for our good and for His glory, even in our trials. He's in the stands, and He doesn't miss a single play. He's cheering us on. He doesn't throw His hands up when we falter. He instantly urges us to get back up and keep going.

> **God is watching for your blessing and benefit.**

Nehemiah was an exiled Jew in Persia who became the king's cupbearer. Nehemiah had to take a sip of whatever the king was drinking before he drank it. A few anxious moments would pass, and if Nehemiah didn't keel over dead, the king took his own drink. This story illustrates God's watching over Nehemiah and guiding him to the special purposes He had designed for his life. Nehemiah's favorite prayer habit was to ask God to remember him (see Neh. 5:19; 13:14,22,31). It was as if he were asking, "Keep watching me, Lord." Nehemiah didn't think he had to remind God to watch him because He might forget. More likely, Nehemiah was reminding himself that he was speaking to a watching God. These were the prayers of someone whose heart was determined not to falter but to move forward under God's watchful eye.

How do you want God to remember you today as He watches over your life? Write your ideas and then lift them to God as a prayer.

Practice this week's memory verse, 1 Corinthians 10:13, by writing it here.

Day 4

HOW GOD WATCHES US

Today's Scripture Focus

"The eyes of the LORD run to and fro throughout the whole earth,
to give strong support to those whose heart is blameless toward him."

2 Chronicles 16:9

God knows, He sees, and nothing is hidden from His sight.

It's important to remember that when we use phrases like "God is watching," God is the overwhelmingly important part of that statement. It changes what we mean by *watching*. God isn't watching us to find out what's going to happen next. He already knows. He's watching because He loves and values us and wants the best for us. God is watching His plan unfold. So when "the eyes of the LORD run to and fro," it doesn't mean God is anxiously trying to take it all in because He doesn't want to miss the occasional person "whose heart is blameless toward him." It means He knows, He sees, and nothing is hidden from His sight.

The power in this verse is the reminder that God doesn't miss anything. He is fully aware. He understands the details, and He assesses things truthfully. When God asks us a question, it's never a good idea to start with "Well, it's complicated, Lord." That may be a problem for us that we have probably created; it's not a problem for Him. In the time of the events of 2 Chronicles, several dozen kings reigned in Israel, counting both the Davidic kingdom of Judah in the south and the 10 tribes in the north. Every king got one of two report-card grades: A if he did right in the sight of the Lord or F if he did evil in the sight of the Lord. It was pass or fail, and most of them failed.

In the context of today's Scripture focus, God was dealing with King Asa, who was doing evil in God's sight. God sent the king a prophet who announced the promise and then pointed out to the king, "Sorry, you're not among those whose hearts are blameless toward God; there's going to be trouble." Years before, Asa had made some effort to rule according to God's laws, but he made the mistake of forgetting that God was watching. When God intervened to keep him from faltering, Asa took the wrong course. The prophet rendered God's judgment: "Because you relied on the king of Syria, and did not rely on the LORD your God, the army of the king of Syria has escaped you" (2 Chron. 16:7). Instead of repenting, Asa became enraged and turned his back on the Lord. His remaining years were spent inflicting cruelty on his people, battling other nations, and enduring illness (see vv. 9-12).

Fortunately for us, the promise that was held out to Asa and rejected is still held out to us. We don't have to falter. God is watching "to give strong support to those whose heart is blameless toward him" (v. 9).

What help does 2 Chronicles 16:9 promise to prevent us from faltering?

What does the verse identify as your role in not faltering?

Valued and Precious

God's eyes are on us as He seeks our welfare. Isaiah 43:3-4 explains why:

> "I am the LORD your God,
> the Holy One of Israel, your Savior.
> I give Egypt as your ransom,
> Cush and Seba in exchange for you.
> Because you are precious in my eyes,
> and honored, and I love you,
> I give men in return for you,
> peoples in exchange for your life."

God was declaring to His chosen people that He had been willing to sacrifice several nations in the process of redeeming Israel. He said Israel was precious and honored in His eyes, and He loved them. He looks at us the same way.

In the previous verses underline words that reveal the way God looks on His children.

What are some things we consider precious that God doesn't value?

How do you know you are precious to God?

You aren't precious because you have value. You are precious because God values you.

Precious is a word that expresses value. Money isn't precious; there's plenty of money around. Education isn't precious; educated fools are practically a proverb. But God says, "You are precious in my eyes." You aren't precious because you have value. You are precious because God values you. He redeemed Israel with other nations. He redeemed you with His Son. God has set a value on you that is not intrinsic to you. He has chosen to love you: "He chose us in him before the foundation of the world" (Eph. 1:4). Your value is based on what God has said about you. You didn't earn it or deserve it; you also can't lose it or forfeit it. God has determined your value. He has declared you priceless. When God says you are precious, that's a promise you can treasure.

The Watcher's Agenda

Because God has declared us precious and honored, He keeps His eye on us. Yesterday we learned that God isn't watching to catch us when we falter; He's watching to keep us from faltering. He has our best interests in mind and heart. His watchfulness is flavored with goodness—always. Here are some ways God watches for our good.

The eyes of the Lord are inescapable. Read the following verses.

> "A man's ways are before the eyes of the LORD,
> and he ponders all his paths." *Proverbs 5:21*

> "The eyes of the LORD are in every place,
> keeping watch on the evil and the good." *Proverbs 15:3*

God sees all of our paths, and His eyes are "in every place." God sees it all because He's watching.

The eyes of the Lord are synonymous with what is right and true. Deuteronomy 6:18 says, "You shall do what is right and good in the sight of the LORD, that it may go well with you." In the Old Testament we read about kings of Israel who did what was right in the eyes of the Lord and others who did not. The eyes of the Lord are synonymous with what is right and true, constantly gazing on us and leading us toward what is good.

> **The eyes of the Lord are synonymous with what is right and true, constantly gazing on us and leading us toward what is good.**

The eyes of the Lord are focused on and attentive to His own. Imagine your neighborhood for a moment from a Google Earth perspective. God is looking down at your block and knows the houses in which His children live. Although God sees everything that happens on your street, He has a predisposition to fix His attention on what's going on in the lives of His children and to extend His loving care toward us. His watching is not a zoomed-out glance from 30,000 feet; He is very focused on His own. First Peter 3:12 says, "The eyes of the Lord are on the righteous and his ears are open to their prayer. But the face of the Lord is against those who do evil." Because you love Christ, God pays attention to you in a special and specific way.

The eyes of the Lord are searching for people to bless. God is looking for people on whom to show His favor. That's the message of 2 Chronicles 16:9, our Scripture focus today. He's watching "to give strong support to those whose heart is blameless toward him." He's looking for people who want to experience His strength. He never gets tired of picking out His children in the crowd with whom He can be pleased and on whose behalf He can show Himself strong.

The eyes of the Lord are provoked to grace when He observes a righteous person. Genesis 6:8 says, "Noah found grace in the eyes of the Lord" (NKJV). What a great challenge. I hope when God sees you and me, He says, "Get more blessing over to that child; He loves My Son. Help her; she's following My way."

Check the characteristic of God's watching that you find most encouraging for your walk with God. If you are faltering in your faith or in a particular aspect of your Christian life, select the characteristic you will claim as a promise. Read the Scripture verses associated with that promise.

- ☐ The eyes of the Lord are inescapable (see Prov. 5:21; 15:3).
- ☐ The eyes of the Lord are synonymous with what is right and true (see Deut. 6:18).
- ☐ The eyes of the Lord are focused on and attentive to His own (see 1 Pet. 3:12).
- ☐ The eyes of the Lord are searching for people to bless (see 2 Chron. 16:9).
- ☐ The eyes of the Lord are provoked to grace when He observes a righteous person (see Gen. 6:8).

Ask God to show you what He sees in your life when His eyes "run to and fro throughout the whole earth, to give strong support to those whose heart is blameless toward him" (2 Chron. 16:9). What evidence do you see in your life that God is supporting you because your heart is blameless toward Him?

What evidence do you see that indicates you are faltering in your faith?

Thank God for the instances of His support you can see. Ask Him to point out in you anything preventing your heart from being blameless toward Him. If you need to repent, read 1 John 1:5-10 and spend time confessing and repenting of your sin.

Recite this week's memory verse, 1 Corinthians 10:13.

Day 5

A WAY OF ESCAPE

Today's Scripture Focus

"No temptation has overtaken you that is not common to man.
God is faithful, and he will not let you be tempted beyond
your ability, but with the temptation he will also provide
the way of escape, that you may be able to endure it."
1 Corinthians 10:13

This week we have learned that God is watching you for your blessing and your good. His heart is inclined toward you, and He wants you to succeed in the Christian life. He wants to support you so that you will not falter. Considering His great love for you, do you honestly think He would let you go through more than you can handle? No. He won't let the waters drown you. He will keep the fires from burning you. He won't allow any trial to knock you off the path.

Trials and Temptations

Today's Scripture focus is one of the greatest promises in God's Word. In Greek, the original language of the New Testament, there is just one word for *temptation* and *trial*. The same word is used interchangeably for both meanings, based on the intent of the passage. The context of 1 Corinthians 10:13 allows us to use both meanings of the word. God isn't going to allow either a temptation or a trial in your life that He won't equip you to handle.

What would you say is the difference between a temptation and a trial?

Temptation is a solicitation to do evil. It comes from Satan and is meant to pull you down. James 1:13 tells us, "[God] himself tempts no one." But a trial? That comes from God. He brings circumstances into your life or allows them to happen to increase your faith in Him and to transform you into the likeness of Jesus. God uses trials to make you better. First Corinthians 10:13 promises that neither a temptation nor a trial is going to overtake your life.

As you think about a difficult situation in your life, would you say it is a temptation or a trial? How do you know?

> God isn't going to allow either a temptation or a trial in your life that He won't equip you to handle.

If it is a trial, how are you yielding yourself to God so that He can strengthen your spiritual walk through this experience?

No matter what's happening under your roof, you should believe God is watching, and as today's Scripture focus asserts, "God is faithful." Make a habit of asserting God's faithfulness in every circumstance. You don't know what's going to happen today, but you need to believe God will be faithful. You can trust that He will not allow you to be tried beyond your ability to withstand. That's called faith! When you're exercising it, you won't falter.

> Make a habit of asserting God's faithfulness in every circumstance.

How are you asserting God's faithfulness in the way you approach your trial or temptation?

Ways of Escape

Today's Scripture focus says when are tempted or tried, God "will also provide the way of escape, that you may be able to endure it" (1 Cor. 10:13). Here are some off-ramps He may provide.

God might end the trial now. He can pull you right out of the fire: "That's enough. You've learned it. I've been glorified in it. It's over." When God moves, the mountains get leveled, the floods get lowered, and the sun suddenly breaks through. Persevere, and you will see God work on your behalf.

In Acts 16 Paul and Silas had been imprisoned in Philippi. During the night as they were praying and singing hymns, "suddenly there was a great earthquake, so that the foundations of the prison were shaken. And immediately all the doors were opened, and everyone's bonds were unfastened" (v. 26). God directly intervened to end Paul and Silas's trial.

God might give you encouragement to keep going. God will send some people to pray for you. I remember going through a very difficult month a while back. But every week four or five pastor friends of mine from other parts of the country called me on the phone: "James, you've been on my heart, and I don't know why. I just want you to know I love you and I'm praying for you." That welcome encouragement was a way of escape for me. God prompts people's hearts so that they pray for you, and their prayers give you the power to persevere.

God also provides encouragement by providing someone to share the burden, a brother or a sister who really knows what your struggle is like. You feel your load lightened when they are around because you realize, *I'm not alone in this trial.*

Just after the apostle Paul became a believer, he was led to Damascus to be discipled by Ananias. When the Jews plotted to kill him, Paul's new Christian friends helped him escape to Jerusalem (see Acts 9:23-25). Later Acts 12 records that King Herod had Peter arrested. However, the church in Jerusalem earnestly prayed for him, and God sent an angel to lead him past the guards and out of prison (see vv. 1-11). In both cases God used the body of Christ to provide prayer support and a practical means of help in hardship.

> **Do you have people praying for you in what you are going through? If not, ask someone to walk with you through this trial and to support you by listening, offering encouragement, and praying.**

God gives you wisdom to act. Sometimes God relieves your hardship by giving wisdom and direction. You don't know what to do, but God gives you wisdom if you ask Him: "If any of you lacks wisdom, let him ask God, who gives generously to all without reproach, and it will be given him" (Jas. 1:5). When God shows you a new angle on your problem, that can change everything.

God had big plans to use Moses to deliver His people from bondage in Egypt. But when Moses was still a baby, Pharaoh gave orders for the midwives to kill all male Hebrew children. However, two midwives feared God and let the babies live. When Pharaoh questioned them, they responded, "The Hebrew women are not like the Egyptian women, for they are vigorous and give birth before the midwife comes to them" (Ex. 1:19). God gave these women wisdom to make the right decision and then to stand up for their actions. Their response preserved not only their own lives but also the life of the future deliverer, Moses.

God gives you strength to persevere. There are days you don't think you will be able to get through. But God gives you His strength to keep going: *I thought I couldn't take it anymore; I can't believe how God has energized me for a new season of faithfulness. I know this didn't come from me.*

When Paul wrote 2 Corinthians, he described a time on his journey to Asia when he and his partners were persecuted. He wrote, "We were so utterly burdened beyond our strength that we despaired of life itself. Indeed, we felt that we had received the sentence of death" (2 Cor. 1:8-9). Paul's description indicates that they were at the end of their rope, without strength or resources. But they

When God shows you a new angle on your problem, that can change everything.

responded to this trial not by relying on their own strength "but on God who raises the dead" (v. 9), and He delivered them from danger.

God gives you a few days of relief. Getting away can give you an oasis in the middle of the desert, renewing your strength. Never underestimate the power of silence in God's presence as He draws near to you when no one else is around.

Even Jesus sought moments of solitude and refreshment. Luke 6:12 records that He spent all night in prayer before choosing the twelve apostles.

Describe a time when God provided one of the previous off-ramps to give you relief in a hard circumstance. What solution did He provide?

When we talk about a way out, keep in mind that we are referring to a way God provides to accomplish His will and to carry you through in victory. We aren't talking about indulging in various forms of escapism, tuning out through irresponsibility, or ending your life. If God has allowed a trial in your life, He has a purpose He wants to bring about through it. You don't have the option of circumventing His plan unless you choose to go outside His will. You don't want to do that. No matter how bad the situation, God can get you through it. Because He is watching, He knows what you are going through. He will go through it with you. That's His promise, and it's always true.

> Because God is watching, He knows what you are going through. He will go through it with you.

How might your approach to your trial change if you truly believed—

God is watching and knows what you are going through?

God is going with you through the fire?

God will not let you falter if you place your faith in Him?

God will provide a way of escape to help you endure?

Spend time in prayer thanking God that He is faithful and is watching. Express your trust in Him to carry you through your trial and to provide a way of escape through intervention, encouragement, wisdom, strength, or a respite. Ask Him to help you submit to His purposes in allowing this trial in your life and to grow your faith in and dependence on Him.

Recite this week's memory verse, 1 Corinthians 10:13.

Week 6

I WILL NOT FAIL
GOD IS ALWAYS
VICTORIOUS

This Week's Promise

I will not fear; God is always with me.

I will not doubt; God is always in control.

I will not despair; God is always good.

I will not falter; God is always watching.

I WILL NOT FAIL; GOD IS ALWAYS VICTORIOUS.

This Week's Memory Verse

" 'No weapon formed against you shall prosper,
And every tongue which rises against you in judgment
You shall condemn.
This is the heritage of the servants of the Lord,
And their righteousness is from Me,'
Says the Lord." *Isaiah 54:17, NKJV*

Finishing Well

Hawaii, one of the most beautiful places on earth, is the site of a volcanic crater called Haleakala. With a circumference of 21 miles, the crater is 7 miles long and 2,600 feet deep. One morning while we were visiting Hawaii, we took a van to the top of the volcano before sunrise. As the sun crept up over the far side of the crater, the beauty of God's creation was stunning. The psalmist must have been similarly awestruck by the majesty of a scene like that when he wrote,

> "From the rising of the sun to its setting,
> the name of the LORD is to be praised!" *Psalm 113:3*

The same power God displayed in creation extends to His promises for the trials we face in life. Even though we are tried and tempted in many ways, God's promises assure us that we are not going to fail.

At the end of the day, the difficult thing about trials is the not knowing. The reason we fear and doubt, despair and falter is that we don't know how it's all going to end. Just test me on this one. Think of a situation that keeps you awake at night. Get in your mind the issue that lingers on the edges of your thoughts and never fully goes away. If you definitively knew right now how that circumstance was going to end, you think you would be OK. If you could foresee it ending well, you could bear the waiting. If you saw it ending badly, you could prepare yourself for what's to come. It's the not knowing that makes you crazy.

One of the revealing and hopeful notes on failure in the Bible comes from Peter's crash-and-burn experience when, in the space of a couple of hours, he went from pledging dying allegiance to Jesus to swearing he didn't know the man. God was watching all of that. Jesus even warned Peter—but what a warning! "Simon, Simon, behold, Satan demanded to have you, that he might sift you like wheat, but I have prayed for you that your faith may not fail. And when you have turned again, strengthen your brothers" (Luke 22:31-32). Jesus foresaw Peter's failure and beyond. As long as Peter was willing to turn and open himself to Jesus' restoration, his failure wasn't final.

Similarly, our trials—our fears, doubts, despair, faltering, and failures—aren't terminal unless we try to resolve them alone and with our own resources. If we believe God's promises to meet our needs and if we remain open to the ways He wants to work through these situations, His ultimate victory can be ours, even if we have our share of stumbling along the way.

Week 6

GROUP EXPERIENCE

On the Same Page

1. In what sports is it possible to lose along the way and still win?

2. React to the following definition. Training is the calculated endurance of defeats on the way to victory. For example, in training to run a marathon, how many marathons do you run? How can even defeats teach us to succeed if we don't allow them to defeat us?

Preparation and Review

1. Share ways you have applied one of the four promises we've already studied to a situation in your life.

2. What do you think it means to experience victory in the Christian life?

3. Together read aloud this week's memory verse on page 132.

DVD Session 6 Viewer Guide

At the end of the day, it's the _not knowing_ that crushes.

The promises are the _knowing_ in the place of the not knowing.

We all live with a certain amount of _uncertainty_.

"No weapon formed against you shall _prosper_" (Isa. 54:17, NKJV).

Nothing ultimately used against you will _triumph_ or _prosper_.

The Lord _fights_ for you.

"Every _tongue_ which rises against you in judgment you shall _condemn_" (Isa. 54:17, NKJV).

"Their ___righteousness___ is from Me" (Isa. 54:17, NKJV).

In ___Christ___ you have a righteousness that is not your ___own___.

"The God of peace will soon crush ___Satan___ under your feet" (Rom. 16:20).

Promise 5: I will not ___fail___; God is always ___victorious___.

Ultimate victory:

His ___purposes___ will be accomplished, His enemies will be defeated, the faithful will be rewarded, His ___son___ will be on the throne established forever, and death itself will be defeated and ended for all time.

You cannot make complete sense of the events of life without the reality of ___eternity___.

You can't fully make sense of the events of life without a true comprehension of the reality of ___heaven___ and ___hell___.

Genesis 3:15
Isaiah 14:16
Revelation 20:10

Responding to the DVD Teaching

1. What are some things you don't know about the road ahead that sometimes trouble you?

2. Based on Romans 16:20, how does focusing on Christ's eventual victory and your share in it help you in your daily living?

3. How has this study of God's promises given you a different understanding of His involvement in your life?

**Read week 6 and complete the activities to complete your study of *Always True*.
Read and recite this week's memory verse, Isaiah 54:17, at least once each day this week.**

This video session is available for download at *www.lifeway.com/alwaystrue*.

I WILL NOT FAIL

Today's Scripture Focus

" 'No weapon formed against you shall prosper,
And every tongue which rises against you in judgment
You shall condemn.
This is the heritage of the servants of the LORD,
And their righteousness is from Me,'
Says the LORD."
Isaiah 54:17, NKJV

Every assertion we have made in this study of God's promises means very little if the related statement about God is not absolutely true. God always keeps His end of the agreement. If there is any uncertainty, it's on our end.

Try to complete the five beliefs and promises you have studied.

1. I will not ~~fer~~ fear ; God is always with me .

2. I will not _____; God is always in _____.

3. I will not _____; God is always _____.

4. I will not _____; God is always _____.

5. I will not fail; God is always victorious.

Check your answers against the list on page 132.

God always keeps His end of the agreement.

No Weapon Shall Succeed

God gave today's Scripture focus to the Israelites as they came home after being in Babylonian captivity. Judgment was over, and now blessing was coming. God gave them a promise that begins, "No weapon formed against you shall prosper" (NKJV). In the Hebrew language *weapon* means *any tool or utensil used against a person.* A weapon is anything used against someone for evil intent.

God extends this promise by grace to all of His children. Nothing "formed against you shall prosper" (NKJV). The word *prosper* gives us hope. The English

Standard Version uses the word *succeed*, and the New International Version says *prevail*. Nothing built, sharpened, aimed, or fired against you, your family, your church family, God's kingdom, or God's people will succeed. If someone uses their wealth, their power, their influence, or their speech against you, it will not succeed. The promise in Isaiah 54:17 gives us confidence to face our struggles.

What weapons are being used against you in a trial or problem you are facing?

Does it appear that you are winning or losing? Why?

The world may not see the truth of this promise. The immediate situation may look like defeat. But God always gets the last word, and He is victorious. God's control and sovereignty are not limited to the spiritual realm. He is sovereign over all weapons. In every way life can be lived calmly and confidently in God's hands.

In spite of the way your present battle appears, no weapon used against you will be final. Things are not over until God says they are over. Even if it looks as if a weapon is prospering or prevailing, the story is not over yet. That weapon may win the battle, but it won't win the war. Satan and the world can measure success only in this world, in the realm of time. But that's just the first inning! The second inning is eternity, and we win. God takes it very seriously when someone opposes or attacks the ones He loves.

> God takes it very seriously when someone opposes or attacks the ones He loves.

Identify the types of attacks believers are experiencing in our world today.

Battles are raging in our world. Weapons are being formed against us. The world is still under the dominion of Satan, and efforts to silence, distort, and distract Christians can be found everywhere. Religions devised by mere humans continue to march against God's revelation and the good news of the gospel. Families and churches are being attacked by discord, sin, and compromise. If you are consistently placing your crisis in God's hands and walking by faith, He promises that none of these attacks can prevail against you.

Fighting the Battle

The weapons we run up against in this world vary. A rumor may seem harmless until you realize your character is under assault. But according to God's promise, weapons of words will not win against you either. Look at the second phrase in Isaiah 54:17:

> "Every tongue which rises against you in judgment
> You shall condemn" (NKJV).

God gives you permission to condemn these attacks, but believers don't condemn as the world does.

- Have you ever been a target for hurtful words because of your stand for the Lord? The way you respond will tell the person your confidence is in God rather than in a need to retaliate.

- Have you experienced ridicule because of your loyalty to Christ? Your gracious but unbending responses may be your finest moments of testimony for Jesus.

- Do you know what it's like to be scorned because of your stand for righteousness? Now you know what it's like to stand with Christ.

- Have you been rebuked because of your fidelity to God's agenda? That rebuke is a weapon that will not prosper.

These are ways believers condemn those who attack them for their testimonies. If you said no to the previous questions, that's not a good sign. It most likely means the people around you haven't noticed any direct connection between you and God. Paul wrote to Timothy, "All who desire to live a godly life in Christ Jesus will be persecuted" (2 Tim. 3:12). If we never risk standing for Christ, we will never discover the faithfulness of God's promises.

If we never risk standing for Christ, we will never discover the faithfulness of God's promises.

Is your trial being caused by your stand for Christ? If so, explain how.

How has your response condemned the attacks of your enemies?

Our society automatically questions anyone who not only claims to be a Christian but also takes seriously the words of Christ. If you do that, don't be surprised if you are labeled as a borderline fanatic. Isn't it interesting that society lauds someone who sells out for a diet, sports team, or wacky television contest but ridicules someone who stands for the truth? The weapons of the world will be effective only if we allow them to keep us silent. The promise of Isaiah 54:17 suggests that faithfulness to God is victory, no matter what else happens.

In your current trial or hardship what weapons of the world are you concerned about?

How does God's promise in Isaiah 54:17 help you stand in faith against those weapons?

Holy Boldness

For many people it's a stretch to assert, "I will not fail." Why is that? If we're trying to generate certainty and confidence in our ability to succeed in the Christian life, this is going to end up being an empty or obnoxious claim, no matter how we say it. The wherewithal not to fail isn't in us; it's in God.

> The wherewithal not to fail isn't in us; it's in God.

When Joshua took over leadership from Moses to take the people of Israel into the promised land, he had big sandals to fill. We think of him as young, but he wasn't that young any more—maybe in his 60s. Moses gave him good advice, and he got to observe the great leader's example for more than 40 years. And when it was Joshua's turn to take the helm, God told him:

> "Be strong and courageous, for you shall cause this people to inherit the land that I swore to their fathers to give them. Only be strong and very courageous, being careful to do according to all the law that Moses my servant commanded you. Do not turn from it to the right hand or to the left, that you may have good success wherever you go. This Book of the Law shall not depart from your mouth, but you shall meditate on it day and night, so that you may be careful to do according to all that is written in it. For then you will make your way prosperous, and then you will have good success." *Joshua 1:6-8*

Did you notice God's idea of "strong and very courageous"? It meant "being careful to do according to all the law that Moses my servant commanded you." To stay strong and courageous for the long haul, Joshua would have to employ three core spiritual disciplines.

1. "This Book of the Law shall not depart from your mouth." This means, "Don't stop talking about My Word."

2. "Meditate on it day and night." Meditating on and memorizing God's Word are sure ways to let it saturate and transform our minds.

3. "Be careful to do according to all that is written in it." God was saying if we know His Word, recognize the applications of it, and obey it, we will not fail.

How was obedience to God's Word going to be the key to Joshua's success?

How does a reliance on God's Word give believers boldness today?

In what ways do you need boldness to deal with your particular trial or problem?

As we face our trials, God's Word arms us for battle by giving us boldness and confidence in the One who has promised that we will not fail. When a Christian church is firebombed by the enemies of our Lord, do you think those believers have failed? God says, "No weapon formed against you shall prosper" (Isa. 54:17, NKJV). You will not fail in spiritual warfare. Your faith in God and your obedience to His Word will arm you for every battle.

Your faith in God and your obedience to His Word will arm you for every battle.

Ask God to give you a heart to believe His promises and boldness to stand on His Word as you face attacks by the weapons of this world.

Begin memorizing this week's memory verse, Isaiah 54:17.

Day 2

GOD, MY VICTORY

Today's Scripture Focus

"God considers it just to repay with affliction those who afflict you."

2 Thessalonians 1:6

Yesterday you learned that the weapons of this world will not succeed against someone who stands with Christ. Those who rise against you won't have the last word. Today's Scripture focus says God will have the final say. Is someone making it hard for you? Resisting you? Challenging you? Someday God will repay them for persecuting you, and you will be able to affirm, "God's Word has proved itself true. I wasn't foolish to trust the Lord Jesus Christ." The slanderers will be silenced, conclusively proved to be in error and justly condemned. If you've experienced pain from others who oppose you and God's will for your life, God's promise is that you will not fail. Why? Because the victory is His.

Jesus Has Overcome

When God promised, "No weapon formed against you shall prosper" (Isa. 54:17, NKJV), He didn't mean we can get rid of threats like dangerous weapons while we are on planet Earth. These things are part and parcel of living in a fallen world. The elimination of one weapon would lead to the arrival of several more. The promise isn't for a safe world but for a God who is able to protect and prevent such weapons from prospering against us.

> **The promise isn't for a safe world but for a God who is able to protect and prevent such weapons from prospering against us.**

The same is true of weapons that come against us in spiritual battles. The issues we are examining in this study—fear, doubt, despair, faltering, and failure—are the stuff of engagement with life. God has not promised to obliterate these enemies during our earthly lives. However, we have the assurance of the words Jesus spoke to the disciples at the Last Supper: "I have said these things to you, that in me you may have peace. In the world you will have tribulation. But take heart; I have overcome the world" (John 16:33).

Check the statements that are true.

☐ Jesus destroyed any expectations for peace on earth.

☐ Jesus said we will have problems while we are on earth.

☐ Jesus said to place our hopes for peace in Him.

First Jesus destroyed any false expectations for His followers' walks with Him. We will have trouble as long as we are on this earth. So we're going to need some help, some promises, and some backup. Jesus came through on this front big-time. He declared victory: "Take heart; I have overcome the world."

Jesus said He has already overcome the world, yet we still encounter evil and experience suffering. Explain what you think Jesus' words mean.

Jesus came to earth to defeat sin and death, your ultimate enemies. He did this by dying on the cross as the perfect sacrifice for humanity's sin and by rising from the dead. These deeds are accomplished facts. The victory is already won. When the time is right, He will return to judge evil, establish His kingdom, and end the curses of sin and death forever.

Jesus' victory is not just ultimate. As long as we are on earth, skirmishes go on in individual lives, families, neighborhoods, cities, and countries; we live in a spiritual war zone. Ephesians 6:12 tells us, "We do not wrestle against flesh and blood, but against the rulers, against the authorities, against the cosmic powers over this present darkness, against the spiritual forces of evil in the heavenly places." Yet Jesus' victory is real. He lives within believers to give us daily victories over sin and evil. It's more than just getting through a crisis. It's walking in faith and victory with our living Savior and Lord.

> It's more than just getting through a crisis. It's walking in faith and victory with our living Savior and Lord.

How does it change your perspective on your trial to know that Jesus has already won the victory?

Our Landmark

Psalm 121:1-2 begins,

> "I lift up my eyes to the hills.
> From where does my help come?
> My help comes from the LORD,
> who made heaven and earth."

People who travel in the wilderness and don't want to get lost know they have to lift their eyes and aim for a distant landmark. As long as they keep the landmark in sight, they will head in the right direction. For believers, God's victory is our landmark. That's where we're headed. We may be scrambling over boulders and walking around chasms, but we're also watching where we're headed—victory with Christ. We can endure hard days, weeks, months, years, and even decades because we know how it ends: God is victorious. So we always have hope. Paul expressed it like this: "We are always of good courage. We know that while we are at home in the body we are away from the Lord, for we walk by faith, not by sight. Yes, we are of good courage, and we would rather be away from the body and at home with the Lord. So whether we are at home or away, we make it our aim to please him" (2 Cor. 5:6-9). The landmark we are using doesn't allow us to walk by sight. We must trust the promise of God's victory and walk by faith.

How does God's eventual victory function as a landmark for your faith?

We can endure hard days, weeks, months, years, and even decades because we know how it ends.

As believers we learn, like Paul, to live with two realities in mind: we are home here in the body, and we anticipate being home with Christ. Anticipation of that future life with Christ should infuse our earthly life with hope and victory. We should seek to obey God and make ourselves available for His use and for His glory. We should rejoice that every time God is glorified in and through our lives, victory has come about. The victorious Christian life is not our boasting of spiritual prowess but Christ living through us to make us more like Him and to be expressions of His love and grace in this world.

Most of us will never have more than a taste of the trials and temptations Job faced. The losses he suffered and the pain he endured were off the charts. He played in a league of his own, and we wouldn't qualify as water assistants for his team. But that doesn't mean we can't learn from his suffering.

At one point in his intense conversations with the three friends who came to straighten him out, Job asserted this amazing understanding of the big picture:

> "He knows the way that I take;
> When He has tested me, I shall come forth as gold." *Job 23:10, NKJV*

"He knows the way that I take" is a brilliant summary of every assertion we've made about God in this study of His promises. We might say, "He who is always with me, always in control, always good, always watching, and always victorious knows the way that I take." Job may have had his share of questions and frustrations, but he knew God. He also knew that whatever he was going through was subject to a schedule, a timeline: "When He has tested me. ..." He was in it and under it, but at some point it would be over.

God's victory isn't just cosmic; it's personal. The more we become saturated with the promise of God's victory, the more that victory becomes ours. That's when we can state with conviction, "I will not fail; God is always victorious." Job was going for the gold. He knew that's what God was going for in him, so he was willing to walk by faith in that direction.

What would coming forth as gold from a difficult trial look like to you?

What glimpses of gold are you beginning to see in your walk with Christ? Check any areas of life in which you are seeing victory.

- ☐ Character, growth in Christlikeness
- ☐ Intimacy with the Lord
- ☐ Ability to obey
- ☐ Love for others
- ☐ Faith in God's promises
- ☐ A life that brings glory to God
- ☐ Desire to minister
- ☐ Desire to worship
- ☐ Response to a trial in your life
- ☐ Other:

Praise God for the victory He has already won through His Son. Express your faith in Him to give you victory as you believe His promises for your trials.

Practice this week's memory verse, Isaiah 54:17.

> The more we become saturated with the promise of God's victory, the more that victory becomes ours.

Day 3

GOD FIGHTS FOR YOU

Today's Scripture Focus

"The Lord has driven out before you great and strong nations.
And as for you, no man has been able to stand before you to this day.
One man of you puts to flight a thousand, since it is the Lord
your God who fights for you, just as he promised you.
Be very careful, therefore, to love the Lord your God."

Joshua 23:9-11

Today's Scripture focus recounts the way God fought for His people as they invaded and conquered the promised land. The accounts of the physical battles of the Old Testament can shed light on the spiritual battles described in the New Testament. Joshua reminded the people of Israel that God had fought for them, just as He had promised to do. In the New Testament Paul likewise admonished the Ephesian believers, "Be strong in the Lord and in the strength of his might. Put on the whole armor of God, that you may be able to stand against the schemes of the devil" (Eph. 6:10-11).

> Joshua reminded the people of Israel that God had fought for them, just as He had promised to do.

If you are going through a trial, what are signs of spiritual warfare in your situation?

Read Ephesians 6:13-17 in your Bible. List the six components of God's spiritual armor.

1.

2.

3.

4.

5.

6.

If Joshua could visit with Christians today, he would remind us, "Listen, troops! You're involved in a spiritual battle with Satan, but don't ever forget that the outcome of the battle is in God's hands. He fights for you today just as surely as He fought for us in the promised land."

Wrestling with the Enemy

"We do not wrestle against flesh and blood, but against . . . the spiritual forces of evil" (Eph. 6:12), Paul wrote, using one of the original Olympic sports as an example. Wrestling is a team sport in which a certain number of teammates may lose matches and yet the team still wins. In fact, sometimes the difference is measured not in wins and losses but in how badly a team member loses.

High-school wrestling teams are often challenged to provide competitors on either end of the weight spectrum. They may find it difficult to find a 98-pound freshman who is willing to undergo the hardship and discipline of the sport. Sometimes wrestling teams can also lack a true heavyweight. It's not unusual for the heavyweight match to feature wrestlers who differ in weight by 40 or 50 pounds. The lighter man has his work cut out for him. If he lets the other wrestler fall on him, the match is probably over.

In wrestling the greatest points are achieved by pinning your opponent, immobilizing him on his back. On more than one occasion a contest has been decided in the final match by whether one wrestler pinned the other or merely won the match on points. The picture of a young man valiantly fighting to keep from losing by a pin, even though he has no real hope of winning the match, is an experience in agony and ecstasy. The crowd groans in support as the wrestler strains to resist the weight of a larger man.

On our own we are greatly outmatched against Satan and his forces. We might feel we are fighting a losing battle until we remember nothing we do can contributes to Christ's victory; it is His alone, and He has already accomplished it on the cross. At the same time, our seeming losses will not diminish the sure victory of Christ. Yet He continually encourages us to keep fighting, never settling for failure, right up to the time He consummates His victory. Then the victory becomes ours too. To that end Paul tells us, "Be strong in the Lord and in the strength of his might" (Eph. 6:10). Although we are commissioned to fight, we must never forget that the battle is His.

Although we are commissioned to fight, we must never forget that the battle is His.

Check the statement that describes the way you are approaching your current trial.

☐ I am fighting my own battle by trying to take care of things myself.

☐ I am trusting God to fight my battle for me.

If you are growing in your faith and fighting in God's strength, what victories are you seeing in your life?

The Battle Lines

Joshua said to the nation of Israel, "The LORD has driven out before you great and strong nations. And as for you, no man has been able to stand before you to this day. One man of you puts to flight a thousand, since it is the LORD your God who fights for you, just as he promised you" (Josh. 23:9-10). The enemies may seem daunting to us but not to God. Israel's experience went something like this: they saw the enemy; the enemy saw them—not too impressive; and the enemy saw God, who scared them to death. It wasn't the Israelites who put thousands to flight. We know who caused the enemy to run.

Notice the battle plan Joshua gave the nation of Israel: "Be very careful, therefore, to love the LORD your God" (v. 11). Joshua said to love the One who would fight for them. It's a little unconventional, but it's exactly how the Israelites had defeated Jericho. The people behind the fortified walls of Jericho were hoping the defensive weapons they had formed would prevail against these people whose God had already humiliated the Egyptians and other nations. They were expecting a siege and a fierce battle. What they got was a nation marching around the city praising God. Seven days, lots of trumpet music, and one mighty shout later, the city fell (see Josh. 6:1-20). God decided the victory.

> If you are His child, He's on the front lines battling on your behalf.

God fights for you the same way. If you are His child, He's on the front lines battling on your behalf. Isaiah 54:17 says no weapon will succeed against you. You will condemn "every tongue which rises against you in judgment" (NKJV). God says this is your right and privilege because you are His own:

> "This is the heritage of the servants of the LORD,
> and their righteousness is from Me" (NKJV).

Your righteousness is from the Lord. Maybe you want to object, "I fail the Lord in so many ways. I don't deserve His blessing." Correct, you don't. That's why your righteousness is from Him. As human beings born in sin, we can't generate righteousness on our own. When we accepted Christ, we became righteous in Him. Paul wrote, "For our sake he made him to be sin who knew no sin, so that in him we might become the righteousness of God" (2 Cor. 5:21). Because of Jesus' death on the cross for our sin, we can claim righteousness in Him today. When God looks at us, He sees the righteousness of His beloved Son.

It's for God's glory that you received the righteousness of Christ. It's not because you are something extra special. It's because you are one of God's children, and He has set His love on you. That's why He has won the victory for you, and that's why He continues to fight for you. You can't fail in any spiritual battle if you are claiming the righteousness of Jesus Christ.

> **Write the way you can respond when the Enemy accuses, "You don't deserve to be a righteous child of God."**

The last words of Isaiah 54:17 are "says the LORD" (NKJV). They show up so often in Scripture that we sometimes just glide over them. But God's promises are His words verbatim! We're talking direct quotes. God inserted these little reminders in His Word so that we don't forget to take these promises to heart. We can count on them because they come from the One who can deliver.

> **Describe a way you have seen God fight for you in the past.**

You can't fail in any spiritual battle if you are claiming the righteousness of Jesus Christ.

If you are fighting a spiritual battle you feel you are losing, identify at least one way you will let God fight this battle for you.

☐ I will believe God has promised victory and will fight for me.

☐ I will believe God has set His love on me, and I will love Him more.

☐ I will claim the righteousness of Christ.

Casualties of War

Every soldier knows when he enlists in the armed services, he is agreeing to give his life, if necessary, to defend and serve his country. Similarly, every day somewhere in the world Christians are dying for their faith in Jesus Christ. They are losing their lives, but they are not losing the victory. They may be dead, but they are dead in Christ. Because of their love for Him, these martyrs did not hesitate to exchange their lives on this side of eternity for the joy of seeing others receive the gift of eternal life.

One of the high points of the victory celebration in heaven pictured in Revelation will be the presentation of those who died because of their faith in Christ. Their victory over Satan will be declared in that moment: "They have conquered him by the blood of the Lamb and by the word of their testimony, for they loved not their lives even unto death" (Rev. 12:11).

You may never be called on to give your physical life for the cause of Christ. Nevertheless, every believer must die to the old sinful nature in order to walk with God. Jesus said, "Whoever would save his life will lose it, but whoever loses his life for my sake and the gospel's will save it" (Mark 8:35). Living a life in Christ requires constantly turning away from the flesh, the attractions of the world, and the temptations of the Enemy and embracing a spiritual walk of faith and obedience. This places you in a position to see God fight and win the ultimate victory on your behalf.

Every believer must die to the old sinful nature in order to walk with God.

In prayer turn your life over to God and die to your own desires in the battle you are fighting. Ask Him to show you how to walk with Him in such a way that He fights for you.

Practice this week's memory verse, Isaiah 54:17, by writing it here.

Day 4
GOD ALWAYS WINS

Today's Scripture Focus

"The God of peace will soon crush Satan under your feet.
The grace of our Lord Jesus Christ be with you."

Romans 16:20

The movie *The Passion of the Christ* begins with Jesus' agony in the garden of Gethsemane. As Jesus prays to His Father and sweats drops of blood, Satan is off to one side taunting Him, whispering that the weight is too heavy and the cost is too steep to save humanity.

As Jesus bows to the ground, the camera shifts to the hem of Satan's garment, where a serpent suddenly appears and crawls along the ground toward Jesus. We expect it to strike at any moment. Jesus has just declared, "Not My will, but Yours be done," and the look on His face evokes quiet determination. He stands and, with a last dismissing glance at Satan, suddenly crushes the serpent's head under His sandaled foot.

Our human story started in a garden—the garden of Eden—and took a terrible turn there. The story took a determined turn back in the right direction in the garden of Gethsemane as Jesus accepted the cup of His Father's will and prepared for the cross. The story will come to its eternal conclusion in the garden that makes up the center of the New Jerusalem and surrounds the tree of life—the ultimate victory garden of Jesus Christ.

God always wins! Today's Scripture focus, Romans 16:20, tells us it's going to end like this: "The God of peace will soon crush Satan under your feet." The Enemy's days are numbered. One day your battles with him will come to an end.

Devastating Victory

Romans 16:20 says God's ultimate victory will be realized soon. I think that means sooner than we think. Someday soon we're all going to be in eternity, and we'll be amazed at how fast life raced by. Eternity is rushing on us. This story will soon be in its last and glorious chapter. So anytime it feels as if the time of your trial is dragging by, get in the habit of praying, "Soon, Lord. Soon."

Get in the habit of praying, "Soon, Lord. Soon."

Here's a shocker: God will crush Satan under *your* feet. Think of every battle and struggle you have endured that was prompted by the Enemy of your soul. Every temptation that clawed at you, every painful attack on your body and spirit, all brought on by Satan. Your foot will rise up and crush him. God will make it so.

The first promise in the Bible, Genesis 3:15, foretells that Jesus, the offspring of Eve, will have the final victory over the serpent and will "crush [his] head" (NIV). At the end of time, Satan will be defeated and then cast with all of his demonic hosts into the lake of fire. This is the "second death" (Rev. 20:14).

For us who are in Christ, that final victory means spending forever with the King of kings and Lord of lords. Jesus will deliver "the kingdom to God the Father after destroying every rule and every authority and power" (1 Cor. 15:24). Jesus will reign over His kingdom forever, and those who belong to Him will rule with Him. The eternity Jesus has planned for us is an unlimited capacity to do all to the glory of God. Whether we worship, serve, supervise, create, or just hang out when we are in heaven, we will do all things to the honor of God.

Honoring God Today

There's another side to the reality that the final victory is coming soon: we are running out of time. Our troubles will come to an end before we know it, but so will our opportunities to make a difference on earth.

Our service for our Lord is not limited to eternity. While we are on earth, He expects us to sow seeds that will bear fruit in the form of lives given to Christ, love expressed, hearts cheered, hope offered, and service rendered in Jesus' name. Colossians 3:17 applies to our lives here on earth: "Whatever you do, in word or deed, do everything in the name of the Lord Jesus, giving thanks to God the Father through him." Think about it. Whatever you do today, you have the choice of doing in the name of Jesus. Today is your chance to honor God.

Today is your chance to honor God.

I ran cross-country in high school. There were days when that course seemed so long that I didn't think I could run one more step. But then within an hour, I'd look back and think, *I could have done a little more. I could have gone a little longer.* We all know that feeling. We're in the ultimate race now; it's called life. Before we know it, it's going to be over. I don't want to look back and say, "I could have gone further in my walk with God. What held me back?"

What opportunities to serve Christ have you missed because a hardship has distracted you and dragged you down?

When you consider that your time to serve God on earth is getting shorter, what is one commitment you would like to make to begin serving Him? It may be as simple as encouraging someone who is going through a trial as you are. Ask God to show you how He would like you to honor Him.

We all have uncertainties. We have health concerns. We have burdens in our families and in our marriages and in our careers. We're going through some of the same struggles that people who don't know Christ are going through. The difference is, we have the Lord. We have the Spirit of God alive inside us. We have the grace to love when we're hated. We have the strength to give when we're taken advantage of. We have a supernatural capacity, as one of God's sons or daughters, to live in Christ. We have the promises of God.

Today is your chance to honor God. This is your opportunity to prove the superiority of a life lived in Jesus Christ. Now is the time not to hold back. We need to be running today with our eyes on that final day. Jesus Christ the Lord, who is Himself all of the promises of God, will be forever victorious. The end. We've read to the end of the Book, and God wins.

How are you honoring God in spite of any trials you may be experiencing?

Ask God to help you approach your battles in light of His ultimate victory. Praise Him as the One who has overcome the world. Ask Him to show you how to honor Him as long as you are on earth, even in the way you deal with hardship.

Practice saying this week's memory verse, Isaiah 54:17.

> Jesus Christ the Lord, who is Himself all of the promises of God, will be forever victorious.

Day 5
FROM HERE TO ETERNITY

Today's Scripture Focus

"What no eye has seen, nor ear heard, nor the heart of man imagined,
what God has prepared for those who love him."

1 Corinthians 2:9

It was evening, and the only lights in the room would have been oil lamps and possibly flickering flames in the mud oven in the corner, where earlier the unleavened bread had been baked and the lamb had been roasted in preparation for the Passover. The faces reflecting those simple lights were those of strong, working men, many accustomed to days outdoors on the windswept waves of Galilee. There was something of the troubled waters in those faces that night. With each statement Jesus made, their brows furrowed more in concern, confusion, and a touch of fear. Yet again the One they had seen speak peace to wind and wave and order demons to behave was talking about dying a painful death. Surely such a disaster couldn't be the final outcome of the past three years of wondrous words and works. There must be some other explanation. The nervous men glanced at one another for encouragement but found that the other faces around the table only mirrored their distress.

Then Jesus said, "Let not your hearts be troubled. Believe in God; believe also in me. In my Father's house are many rooms. If it were not so, would I have told you that I go to prepare a place for you? And if I go and prepare a place for you, I will come again and will take you to myself, that where I am you may be also" (John 14:1-3). His disciples' eyes flew open in surprise. They could hardly believe their ears. Their hearts were lifted by His words. Immediately they wanted details on how they could get to the Father's house. Jesus answered in a way they (and we) would never forget: "I am the way, and the truth, and the life. No one comes to the Father except through me" (v. 6). If we want the way to the Father, the truth about the Father, and the life the Father can give us, the source is Jesus. He has promised to come and take us to our eternal dwelling place with Him.

Jesus has promised to come and take us to our eternal dwelling place with Him.

Beyond Our Expectations

The greatest thing about the victory we have in Christ will not be the conclusion of a trial here on earth. It will not be the amazing celebration at the close of the age. The best thing will be the moment we realize we have reached our eternal home with Jesus. After the victory comes the joy of being with the One who made it possible for us to be there. Today's Scripture focus, I Corinthians 2:9, says we can't imagine what it will be like: "What no eye has seen, nor ear heard, nor the heart of man imagined, what God has prepared for those who love him."

Write your favorite idea of heaven you are looking forward to.

How do thoughts of heaven help you deal with hardships here on earth?

The apostle Paul was a little perturbed with his brothers and sisters in Corinth: "It has been reported to me by Chloe's people that there is quarreling among you, my brothers" (I Cor. I:II). Paul knew if these disciples couldn't learn to get along in Christ, they would be woefully ineffective in spreading the gospel. He pointed them toward godly wisdom—the kind found only in Christ: "We preach Christ crucified, … Christ the power of God and the wisdom of God. For the foolishness of God is wiser than men, and the weakness of God is stronger than men" (vv. 23-25). Paul wanted these believers to stop being consumed with the struggles in this life that will be over in a heartbeat. They had taken their focus off the gospel, which brings unity, and had let petty arguments divide them.

Believers today can also get sidetracked and make the immediate more significant than the eternal.

Believers today can also get sidetracked and make the immediate more significant than the eternal. If we let ourselves become more and more earthly minded, we will be less and less effective in accomplishing anything of value for the Kingdom.

List differences between a worldly perspective and an eternal perspective in the following areas.

	Worldly	Eternal
Purpose in life		
Values		

Final destiny

If you are struggling with a trial, how does it tend to distract you from an eternal outlook?

We who are followers of Jesus are challenged to live in the world but not of the world (see John 17:16). We live in a larger world that requires an eternal perspective. All around us are people who can see only the values and ambitions of this world. They are desperate. They have no hope beyond this life. When we take our eyes off the amazing possibilities of glory and all God has prepared for us, focusing instead on this world and all its fallen complications, we lose joy, and we lessen the impact of the gospel for others. That would be a tragic failure.

We have so much more to live for—and that *more* can't be measured in human terms. Paul later wrote, "This light momentary affliction is preparing for us an eternal weight of glory beyond comparison" (2 Cor. 4:17). That's the kind of promise that keeps us focused on the eternal. And when we try to imagine what that "weight of glory" and all "God has prepared for those who love him" (I Cor. 2:9) will look like, we have to conclude that it will be more, better, and beyond—because God has promised to wildly exceed our expectations.

God has promised to wildly exceed our expectations.

How does an eternal perspective help you know what is and isn't important in life?

How does an eternal perspective affect the way you view your trial?

When We All Get to Heaven

Eliza Hewitt and Emily Wilson were Christian friends from different church backgrounds. They met because both of their families vacationed at the same beach community along the eastern shore of the United States. Eliza was the poet of the pair, while Emily was a musician. Their beach retreats were the highlight of each year for these two women, who used the times to encourage each other and share what God had been doing in their lives. One year Eliza brought a poem she had written that reflected her thoughts about believers' shared destination. Emily put it to music, and it became one of those pilgrim hymns that help us lift our eyes and remember that we're looking to a kingdom not of this world but one in the heavens that Jesus has prepared for us. The chorus speaks of the victory that will be ours:

> When we all get to heaven,
> What a day of rejoicing that will be,
> When we all see Jesus,
> We'll sing and shout the victory.

Hymns and praise songs are powerful statements of God's promises. They are testimonies reminding us God is working out His plan for victory. Other believers haven't failed. They claimed God's promises for victory and left us words of encouragement. We won't fail either; God is always victorious!

Name a hymn or praise song that reminds you of Jesus' final victory and our future with Him.

How does this song help give you an eternal perspective on your problems in life?

God's promises continue into eternity.

Promises Kept

As you come to the end of this study, realize that God's promises continue into eternity. They will never stop being true, and they will never fail. God is the great Promise Keeper: "He who calls you is faithful; he will surely do it" (I Thess. 5:24). His great and precious promises are eternally anchored in who He is:

- God makes promises.

- God keeps His promises.

- God wants us to test His promises.

- God's promises are activated by faith.

- God's promises are experienced in Jesus Christ.

God's promises connect the heat and pressure of today with the hope of forever. When things seem dark and hopeless, God's promises intervene with the shining light of God's ultimate victory. They will continually offer you peace that flows from knowing God has all things firmly under control and will bring about His plan in His time. Go to the pages of God's Word and search out the promises He has planted there for you. Drink them in. Meditate on them. Memorize them. Believe them. Stake your life on them. The One who promises is always true.

The One who promises is always true.

Use the five promises as a closing prayer and recite each week's memory verse(s).

Father, thank You for giving me precious and great promises and for always keeping Your promises.	2 Peter 1:3-4
1. I will not fear; You are always with me.	Deuteronomy 31:6
2. I will not doubt; You are always in control.	Proverbs 3:5-6
3. I will not despair; You are always good.	Romans 8:28
4. I will not falter; You are always watching.	1 Corinthians 10:13
5. I will not fail; You are always victorious.	Isaiah 54:17

GOD'S PROMISES ARE
ALWAYS TRUE

Always True
God's Five Promises for When Life Is Hard
James MacDonald

Best-selling author, speaker, and pastor James MacDonald delivers the biblical hope of God's promises in the midst of life's storms. God's promises are great. They don't fall apart during difficult times; they reveal hope in the midst of the storm. And God's promises are precious. They are strong enough to hold you up and resilient enough to get you through.

MacDonald explores five major categories of promises in the Bible and the five areas of life about which God repeatedly makes promises. The Bible has much to say about God's presence in times of difficulty. From fighting fear and doubt to claiming God's goodness, help, and victory, *Always True* will point you to trustworthy promises that will carry you through whatever you are facing in life.

www.moodypublishers.com

ISBN 978-0-8024-5869-8

OTHER STUDIES BY
JAMES MACDONALD

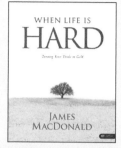

When Life Is Hard

This study explores the scriptural truth that God disciplines all of His children, using trials to train them for their good and for His purposes. Those who submit to God's refining work in their hardship can come forth as gold. Six sessions.

Leader Kit 005271225 • Member Book 005293072

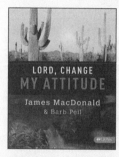

Lord, Change My Attitude

Based on the Israelites' journey out of Egypt, this study shows how attitudes can affect whether someone stays in the wilderness with negative attitudes or enjoys the blessings of the promised land with God-honoring attitudes. Eleven sessions.

Leader Kit 005097385 • Member Book 005035039

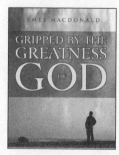

Gripped by the Greatness of God

Based on key teachings from the Book of Isaiah, this study challenges believers to be gripped by God's greatness and to respond to God in worship with renewed zeal, passion, and heartfelt excitement. Eight sessions.

Leader Kit 001288992 • Member Book 001288990

Downpour: He Will Come to Us like the Rain

James MacDonald leads Christians to take the personal steps they need to return to the Lord and experience spiritual renewal and victory. Member book includes a music CD of songs related to the topic. Twelve sessions.

Leader Kit 001303831 • Member Book 001303830

To purchase these resources, write to LifeWay Church Resources Customer Service; One LifeWay Plaza; Nashville, TN 37234-0113; fax (615) 251-5933; e-mail *orderentry@lifeway.com;* phone toll free (800) 458-2772; order online at *www.lifeway.com;* or visit the LifeWay Christian Store serving you.

Two Ways to Earn Credit
for Studying LifeWay Christian Resources Material

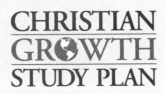

CHRISTIAN GROWTH STUDY PLAN

CONTACT INFORMATION:
Christian Growth Study Plan
One LifeWay Plaza, MSN 117
Nashville, TN 37234
CGSP info line 1-800-968-5519
www.lifeway.com/CGSP
To order resources 1-800-458-2772

Christian Growth Study Plan resources are available for course credit for personal growth and church leadership training.

Courses are designed as plans for personal spiritual growth and for training current and future church leaders. To receive credit, complete the book, material, or activity. Respond to the learning activities or attend group sessions, when applicable, and show your work to your pastor, staff member, or church leader. Then go to *www.lifeway.com/CGSP*, or call the toll-free number for instructions for receiving credit and your certificate of completion.

For information about studies in the Christian Growth Study Plan, refer to the current catalog online at the CGSP Web address. This program and certificate are free LifeWay services to you.

Need a CEU?

CONTACT INFORMATION:
CEU Coordinator
One LifeWay Plaza, MSN 150
Nashville, TN 37234
Info line 1-800-968-5519
www.lifeway.com/CEU

Receive Continuing Education Units (CEUs) when you complete group Bible studies by your favorite LifeWay authors.

Some studies are approved by the Association of Christian Schools International (ACSI) for CEU credits. Do you need to renew your Christian school teaching certificate? Gather a group of teachers or neighbors and complete one of the approved studies. Then go to *www.lifeway.com/CEU* to submit a request form or to find a list of ACSI-approved LifeWay studies and conferences. Book studies must be completed in a group setting. Online courses approved for ACSI credit are also noted on the course list. The administrative cost of each CEU certificate is only $10 per course.